Understanding Your Accounts

For the UK business owner

from.

Perry

Understanding Your Accounts

For the UK business owner

Penny Lowe

Understanding Your Accounts

First published in 2013 by
Anoma Press
48 St Vincent Drive, St Albans, Herts, AL1 5SJ, UK
info@anomapress.com
www.anomapress.com

Book layout by Duncan McKean

Printed on acid-free paper from managed forests. This book is printed on demand to fulfill orders, so no copies will be remaindered or pulped.

Printed and bound by TJ International Ltd, Padstow, Cornwall

ISBN 978-1-908746-60-3

About the Author

Penny originally trained and worked as an accountant/auditor, giving her exposure to a wide variety of industries. She later moved to a growing software and sales company and during her 16 years there, spent time managing many departments including marketing and support. During this time she gained her MBA through the Open University.

She then spent two years working for an American based firm leading a team seconded from various offices around the world and gaining her Prince2 Practitioner in project management. Since 2003 she has headed up Wellington Consulting Ltd, an accountancy practice, management consultancy and training organisation.

Penny has a PGCE teaching qualification and a diploma in coaching. She also runs Wellington Coaching Ltd offering business coaching and mentoring for micro and small businesses.

She loves encouraging people's development and is able to help by use of her coaching and training skills in addition to her technical knowledge. Her practical and honest style is appreciated by delegates, who often comment on the positive change they have undergone as a result of working with her.

Penny is primarily a people person. Her vision is to see individuals and teams become more productive and enjoy what they do.

Foreword

This book is aimed at those who currently run a business, who employ some staff and recognise they could do more, if only they understood the numbers. If you don't already employ staff, read this book anyway. When you do decide to employ them, you will be well prepared.

You don't have to be an accountant to know enough to make a difference. You are already good at understanding what you do for your clients and customers. It's OK to leave much of the number crunching to your book-keeper and accountant. That bit is not what is going to earn the business money (unless you run an accountancy practice in which case this book is for your clients – not you). Understanding the numbers will make a difference to both the turnover and the profit.

This book does not use many manufacturing examples, but what is included will also apply to this type of industry. It assumes that you have goods that you are selling with or without a service attached or you are purely selling a service.

After reading this book, you will understand what the numbers mean, which ones you need to worry about and what questions you should be asking. This added knowledge and understanding will allow you to make the right decisions for your business.

As a business owner, I would encourage you to get involved in the preparation of some of the numbers. You will be able to include facts only known to you, such as when you want to retire or sell the business, to ensure that you achieve your personal and business objectives. You may also know of investors who could support the business through expansion or difficult times. In addition to this, your experience and industry knowledge are likely to be greater than that of the accountant you are working with. You will know about industry trends and what is in the trade journals that may impact on future plans.

Like you, I am always trying to improve. If you want to send me feedback, or share your examples, please leave a message at:

www.understanding-accounts.com/feedback

In summary, you are the key. To open the door, you just need to make sure you are a good fit to unlock the potential of your business.

Contents

1 Why you need to understand the figures

As a business owner, you are responsible for the success or failure of your business. This extends to the effect on anyone you employ, your suppliers, your customers and most of all, you.

When you hear of people talking about you and your business, I am sure that you would like to hear them say: they always pay on time, the level of service is excellent, they can always be relied upon, they charge a fair price, it's a great company to work for. None of these can be achieved unless the hidden challenge of managing your money is being done well.

The phrase CASH IS KING is well known in business because it is so true and has been proved time and time again. Without cash, or funds generally, you cannot continue.

By reading this book, you will fully understand the significance of this phrase and be able to create and maintain a profitable and successful business.

PEOPLE WILL EXPECT YOU TO KNOW YOUR FIGURES

When you are employed, everyone expects that you do your job because you know what you are doing, and are good at it, whether you like it or not. If you are no good, you may get moved within the organisation – or moved out.

Running a business is not quite the same. Only you can decide when to give up. As long as you are running a business, customers, suppliers and staff will expect that you know exactly what you are doing and that anything you do is for the good of the business. The only exception is where there are external shareholders who could vote you out. In this case you are counted as employed – see above.

Being employed, you would have been given the job because you either had the right credentials or you showed an ability to learn. Why did you decide to go into business? Did you study for an MBA and were excited about putting your knowledge into practice by applying the models to your chosen trade or profession? Or did you, as most business owners do, have a desire to provide the best, and possibly most cost effective, solution to customers that will benefit them and you? The solution may be goods, a trade or a service. The same thinking applies to all.

Hopefully you see where I am coming from. The fact you have chosen to run a business leads people to believe you are qualified to do so.

Now for the good news, in the same way large companies have different departments to provide the range of services required by a business, so you can choose to outsource tasks you do not enjoy, or find difficult. To draw a parallel, if you wanted an extension built for your house, you would have a good idea about the size, style, budget and time frame. You would then consult an architect to give you some idea of what is possible/practical, what the local planning and building regulations are, how realistic your budget and time frames are, before deciding whether to go ahead. If you did choose to proceed, you would contract businesses to assist you in achieving your goal of the extension. There are very few of us who would expect to do it all ourselves, from the planning application to the decorating and all that goes on in between.

The important thing to remember is that you had the idea of the extension, but are involving professionals to ensure a successful delivery. It is the same with outsourcing in business. You can call in professionals but you need to know what you want and why – and have an understanding to ensure you get what you want and that the job is done right. Monitoring as the project progresses prevents the need for costly reworks later on.

By understanding the figures, I am not saying you need to dig the foundations and lay the bricks, just agree on what your aims are and have an overall level of knowledge to judge if the wall looks straight and the windows are where they are supposed to be.

When starting out, you may have built your own barbeque in the garden, but my guess is you referred to some form of help or instructions and recognised that this is not on the same scale as an extension: and so it is when beginning in business. By learning the basics and possibly doing them yourself in the very early days, you can understand the big picture without necessarily expecting to do the work as the business grows.

Customers for amended quotes/price deals

Part of every business is selling. Most customers will expect you to understand your costs so that you can be flexible when discussing their requirements.

Have you considered whether it is better to offer two for the price of one, or one at half price? The first will shift the stock and discourage them from looking elsewhere for alternatives until they have used the two you sold them, the latter will reduce the financial outlay required for the customer to take your product but may reduce your income in the current period. Will they also expect a lower price next time? Do you need to shift stock as you can buy more cheaply in bulk and therefore the profit per item is greater if they buy two, even if one is free?

Are you one of those people that stands in a supermarket and works out which of the price deals on a product you want is the most cost effective, or do you judge by the biggest label for savings? One approach takes time and a simple appreciation of the price per gram or unit, e.g. tea bag, the other is an impression given by the marketing material. Which approach do you take?

What do your customers do? One of my clients didn't realise how much he was giving away in discounts until he computerised his accounts function rather than hand-writing customer invoices. When hand-written, it was easy for the customer to offer to pay the figure but rounded down to the nearest ten or hundred pounds. When the invoice is neatly presented by being printed on paper with the logo etc., they expect to pay what is on the invoice – well almost always! The customer assumes that you have accurately costed the job and the price is the price.

Having compared discounts given at point of payment now to when he used the hand-written invoices, he has increased his income just by this one action. The fact is that now he understands that discounts are a cost and will reduce the profit. The added benefit is that the customers respect the fact he has precisely worked out the price. There is little point in challenging it. Also, the customers feel future prices are likely to be consistent as they are calculated not guessed. Actually the prices always were carefully calculated. It is the customer's perception that has changed, and his profits.

Banks for lending, savings, day-to-day account management

Other than the taxman, the other person who will assume you understand your figures is your bank manager. They do not always appreciate that numbers may not be your strong point. What they will expect is that you will have sought help and fully understand your numbers before speaking to them.

When I speak to bank managers, they say they are very frustrated by customers who come to them with either no business plan or a plan provided by someone else that the customer does not understand. Even the basics known in a domestic environment seem to have left the brain when talking about business. If you buy a new TV on credit, you expect to make repayments. If you take out a bank loan, how are you going to find the money for the repayments? When teaching basic book-keeping I often draw a parallel with domestic finances as people often manage those but go into blank mode if you ask them to apply the same thought process to their business.

Bank managers are often criticised for not being prepared to be flexible. Many will be flexible if you give them the answers they want to hear. This includes showing that you understand your business. Not just your speciality and your customers, but when cash comes in and where and when it has to be paid out. This high level view must include saving up for payments to the taxman which catch many businesses out.

The taxman – ignorance is no excuse

Over recent years, HM Revenue and Customs (HMRC) has been generous in agreeing payment terms for outstanding taxes. This has been on the condition you can offer them a plan for repayments and you stick to the plan. Although I say generous, it is actually in their own interest to get some money over a period of time. The alternative would be to receive no money and have to pay the costs incurred in winding up the business.

More recently, HMRC have realised that they have been a cheap form of finance for a business. They are now suggesting that the directors pay the outstanding sums on their personal credit cards or take out personal loans so that the debt is shifted to the business owners rather than HMRC.

Although we are still looking at a high level, it is important to remember that as a business owner you sign the accounts and therefore take responsibility for what they contain. This responsibility is not only the summary figures that may be produced by an external accountant, but also systems and processes behind them. Saying you relied on your accountant is not a defence for not recording the cash that some customers may have given you and therefore did not get entered onto the books. Not having receipts to support payments made or cash coming in is beyond the accountant's control. It is down to you.

If you understand the processes, you can spot where there is an opportunity for error, fraud and theft to occur – and I don't mean by you! The responsibility rests with you, even if you do not do the work.

I had a publican client who initially did not even record his takings. Even when he did start to record them, he never checked his cash against till receipts. He suspected that a member of staff was helping himself from the till but had no way to prove it from his haphazard, almost non-existent book-keeping. One lunchtime, he set a trap by knowing what float was in the till at the start of the shift. He then went out for the afternoon leaving the member of staff to man the pub, as was usual. However, he came back after an hour and checked what was in the till against sales. Surprise, the till was exactly £20 down. The employee resigned on the spot. One wonders how long it had been going on for. The individual is no longer running the pub. I am glad I am not the one having to explain to the taxman why the takings were so low and therefore the payment of VAT and income tax were a lot less than HMRC would have expected. Mismanagement is not an allowable expense and can be viewed as fraud by the taxman. He thinks you should know better and have your own systems in place for your benefit, not just his.

YOU WILL BE LESS VULNERABLE

Another reason why it is useful to understand the figures is that people are less able to take advantage of you. By this I mean blind you with figures. Don't panic, I am not suggesting that you need to know them all intimately, just understand enough.

Going back to my supermarket scenario, if 240 tea bags cost £4.40 and 160 tea bags cost £4.00, you would probably buy the 240 box, but if they offer 'buy 160 and get 40 free', which would you buy?

Price per tea bag:

240 tea bags for £4.40

$$\frac{£4.40}{240} \quad = \quad 1.83\text{p per tea bag}$$

160 tea bags for £4.00

$$\frac{£4.00}{160} \quad = \quad 2.5\text{p per tea bag}$$

160 + 40 free tea bags for £4.00

$$\frac{£4.00}{160+40} \quad = \quad 2\text{p per tea bag}$$

Conclusion: Box of 240 is still the best value

This reason to understand the figures applies as much to you as a customer when you are making purchases for the business, as it does to you as a supplier to your customers.

From customers

If you provide a service, it can be easy for customers to ask 'if you could just ...'. This can be anything from printing off an extra copy to half a day's extra work. If you do not understand your costs, it is difficult to decide what you do as a gesture of goodwill, as opposed to giving an on-the-spot quote so the customer can make a decision as to whether they are prepared to pay that price.

I recently had a fence repaired by one of my clients. As the work was done quickly, I asked if they could also erect a self-assembly chicken house I had not yet got round to constructing. They said they would need to check with the boss. The boss phoned me back and said that his lads could, but as he did not know what was involved, he could not give me a price but as they were on site already, it would be reasonable. I trusted my client and chose to go ahead. He had laid the expectation that I would need to pay for the extra work, and covered his own cost by not giving a wild guess which would either put me off, or be wrong. On the basis of the previous quote for the fence, I was happy to go ahead without an exact figure. The chickens have now moved in.

From suppliers

This can cover anything from advertising being sold over the phone to their obsolete stock being shifted. When someone phones you up with what sounds like a good deal, how do you calculate if it is good for you? When advertisers talk about circulation, do you understand the demographics of your market? You might say this is more to do with marketing than finance. In my opinion it comes back to numbers. If you sell to medium-sized businesses, what benefit would you expect from an advertisement in a free magazine circulated to 24,000 homes in your local area? Would you expect more business to come from distribution to 12,000 businesses? If the advert is going to cost you money, how much money do you expect to make from it? Back to numbers again I'm afraid.

I also referred to deals on stock. If you sell items, how fast does your stock move? If a supplier is off-loading theirs, how quickly are you going to be able to shift it? Are you going to end up paying for storage rather than them? Are they about to publicise a new model so no-one will want to buy the old one? My example used to be the big square computer monitors when the flat screens started to be available. The old screen took a lot of space to store and it wasn't even easy to scrap them. As times move on so does the rate of updating of products and the desire for the latest model. Knowing your numbers will allow you to make the best decisions and not just be drawn to what seems like a good idea.

From staff

This can seem the most threatening. This is not just about staff trying to swindle you, it is about you being the boss.

If someone has part of their income based on commission on sales, is their payment based on invoices raised, or invoices paid? The latter means that they have a greater interest in getting the paperwork right and following up with the new customer to ensure they pay the bill. Putting clauses into staff contracts can heavily influence their attitude to customers and cash.

Another area is expenses. Do your staff know what you count as 'reasonable'? Do they know what is ordered for the office at a discounted price and therefore means they do not need to go to the local shop and pay twice the price? This comes back to you understanding the figures and being prepared to share some of them. The staff can then appreciate why you are creating the rules. In the last example, it also encourages the member of staff who helps themselves to the last one from the cupboard to let someone know that if they expect there to be more later, that stock needs to be re-ordered. It is in their interest so that next time they go to the cupboard there are enough supplies there for them.

My final example is staff theft. Although this is a strong word, that is what it is. Whether it is helping themselves to cash from the till, or selling services that they provide via your company privately to your customers, it amounts to money going into their pocket when it should be in yours. The correct procedure is to let the customer know extra work needed doing, that they can do it, how much it will be and then getting their acceptance that they require the work to be done for the price. Credit where credit is due, we had a gas cooker delivered by Currys and the installer agreed, at a reasonable cost as he was already there, to disconnect an old gas fire and cap the pipe. We agreed the price, paid the extra and got a receipt. I hope the team were congratulated on providing extra services rather than being told they should have made a separate visit which would have bumped up the cost and lost them the business.

By understanding the numbers, you can better explain to staff what is and isn't acceptable – and more importantly why. They are more likely to remember if they understand rather than just being told.

OTHERS UNDERSTAND THEM BETTER THAN YOU

Boards of most large companies will have an accountant as a board member. This suggests that they have a specialist to look in detail at the figures and to explain them to the other board members.

Your business may not yet be this size, but what is true is that all board members should expect to have an understanding of the figures enough to ask questions and potentially challenge the accountant.

They are not expecting to work out the figures themselves, but to have them presented in a way that they can get a feel for the current position, options and implications.

Too scared to ask

When you go to the doctor's, you will describe your symptoms in terms you understand about how you feel. You will not try and put them in the physician's language. The first reason is that you may not know the language, secondly because you run the risk of using the wrong terms or not making yourself clear. If you were a doctor and used the language of your profession to describe your symptoms, the answer may come back in the same language and all would be clear. As you are not a doctor, you may be no wiser.

It really doesn't matter if you use non-accounting terms to ask questions and give answers to others, providing the message is correct and understood by the listener.

If the answers don't make sense to you, it may be the person is not a good communicator or there is a flaw in the figures. You need to ask further questions.

If someone gives you an answer in millimetres when you were expecting centimetres, your brain may simply make the mental adjustments to what it is hearing. However, should you challenge the speaker? If the speaker is talking about price per thousand when they really mean price per hundred, this is only the same factor of ten, but it can have quite an impact on the amount of money needed.

Seeing missed opportunities

It is not always about the figures. Sometimes looking at the figures means you adopt tunnel vision as it may be the only option that you are looking at. Offering an alternative suggestion can be of benefit, but you also need to know how to put figures to these suggestions. You don't need to necessarily work out all the figures, but you need to understand what figures are involved and whether it is worth more detailed calculations.

Seeing the writing on the wall

This can be very telling in some businesses. The staff start to worry, or even leave. The suppliers restrict the credit they give you. Customers start taking advantage of your credit terms and delay paying you. If you are not careful you can start a downward spiral which can be difficult to escape from without drastic action.

By understanding the figures, you will know some of the signs of financial difficulties. The benefit of understanding this is not just to support your own business, but also to make you more aware and on the watch for customers and suppliers experiencing difficulties. This can save you thousands by reducing the possibility of bad debts and making sure you are not paying for goods that are never delivered.

Fraud

I mentioned earlier about a publican who did not record takings and therefore did not know that a member of staff was helping himself out of the till on each shift.

If you do not know what the figures should be, how do you know when they are wrong?

A simple example is the payments that go out of your business bank account. Do you know what each standing order, direct debit and card payment is or are you paying for someone else's eBay purchases? It may not be you that does the checking, but what controls do you have in place?

Who checks the prices on your purchase invoices before they are paid? How do you check that what you are paying for has been received... in full?

How do you control stock? Are your staff or customers helping themselves to stock – or for that matter non-stock items? How many computers are now, and have been, on the books of your business? Do you know where they all are now, or if you have scrapped or sold them? It is not a problem if you no longer have them providing they went with your knowledge and agreement and at a price you have agreed.

Although this just seems to be a series of questions, spotting fraud is a case of knowing what the numbers should be and what they are, then taking action to make sure you stay on track.

Expect you not to be interested

Some business owners claim to not understand the figures. This is often taken as not being interested. There is a big difference. The business owner should want to know whether they would be better to give up and find a job, or whether they can afford to buy themselves a new car or holiday.

Some of this comes back to the style of language used. An accountant may not realise that it is their language that is causing the communication breakdown. This can apply to internal as well as external accountants. When you switch off listening, it is because you don't understand, not because you don't care.

You need to prove to others that although language may be a bit of an initial barrier, it can be broken down, as it is for the common good that you understand the figures.

YOU CAN BE IN CONTROL

Many business owners lose sleep by worrying about their business. The worry may be due to concern about how to pay the bills, pay the staff, obtain money from customers, expand the business. All these boil down to figures.

Once you identify exactly what the type and amount of the concern is, it can then be addressed. It can't necessarily be fixed immediately but it can be quantified and options investigated.

One of my clients called a meeting towards the end of a month, with the staff chasing customers for payment. They were told that in order to avoid wasting money on penalties imposed by HMRC, they needed to collect £15,000 from customers and get it into the bank so that the business could pay all its VAT on the fifth of the next month. They were also given hints and tips such as encouraging customers to pay online. Not only are online payments typically cheaper for both parties, but it does not waste time and effort waiting for the post, going to the bank and then waiting for the cheque to clear. They were briefed that if part of an invoice was in dispute, the customer should be asked to pay the part that is not disputed. Part payment is more acceptable than no payment. A newer member of staff to the team started to understand why 'they said the customer would pay with the next payment run' was not an exact enough answer to ensure that payment would be in the account before the fifth. The money came in, they paid their VAT and they now have better trained staff and an improved system.

The points to note from the above example are that the business owner understood how much he needed and by when (as he had asked, not because he had worked it out). He also understood what the costs would be of not meeting the target, the penalties and the options. One would be that the business owner would have to forego money he would usually expect to draw from the business for himself. The business owner was not their accountant but understood what was needed. He expressed what was needed without the staff having to be accountants or the business owner sounding desperate.

The calm way the problem was presented, together with several approaches to the solution, earned the boss the respect of the staff and their desire to deliver as they understood what they needed to do to achieve the goal and how to do it.

Know the current position

Over and over again I am asked by business owners to coach them. When I ask them to describe the current position, they often flounder. How are they going to judge improvement if they do not have a starting point to measure against?

I would like to increase my sales by 20% is a wonderful goal. But what are we increasing from? What was the increase between last year and the year before – was that an increase of more than 20%? What is the 20% based on? It could be the number of customers, number of units, number of chargeable hours, monetary value of sales, to name a few. Each of these may need to be addressed differently and certainly the starting point needs to be understood.

If you know where you are now, you will also have a history

of how you got there. Depending on how long you have been in business, it may be only a short history. Whatever the length, it allows you to identify trends, whether these are cyclical, marketing-led or something else.

One of my coaching clients engaged me to help her increase her turnover as it was static. She did not know the figures and so her first goal was to work out her sales and costs from 12-15 months ago for that three month period. The next week her goal was updating 9-12 months prior to this period, another three months. She then reported that it hadn't actually been that bad a job once she had started and had blitzed the task, and was now fully up to date. When we compared her current figures to earlier years, there had been a slight growth in turnover – but a greater increase in costs. This is why she had the feeling she needed to do something rather than carry on as she was. She could see that her gut feeling had been right. But increasing the turnover was not going to be enough unless costs were also brought into the equation.

Know what contingencies you have in place

If your suppliers or the tax office want money from you, where will it come from? Some businesses have a bank overdraft, but how close are you to the overdraft limit? Have you got some customers that only pay when they are chased?

Are there any suppliers that could give you a credit account but you have never bothered to apply for it? Although you still need to pay their bills, it may give you breathing space if one customer is being particularly slow – or you have an unexpected expense such as a vehicle repair.

Another facility may be a savings account where you have

put money to one side. OK, but how many smaller businesses feel that they can do this? It may be the tax account that has a balance that you can draw on in the short term providing you repay it. It may be that you have savings and could afford not to pay yourself for a month. Even these small contributions to planning can make a difference.

Know where you are going

In business it can be easy to become overwhelmed by the day-to-day pressures. To know where you are going means you can make decisions which are the best for the business in the long term. I accept that the decision may sometimes mean that you forego long term benefits, but the important thing is that you are making an informed decision.

A friend was offered a job on a salary well under the market rate, but the potential employer offered to review the salary in three months once he knew what impact the new employee was having on the turnover and the bottom line. The business owner had only been running this part of the business for nine months and was right not to overstretch himself until he knew how it was turning out. The employee also has a vested interest in helping the business grow.

BE ABLE TO MAKE INFORMED DECISIONS

As a business leader, the responsibility for the success of the business ultimately rests with you. You can introduce ideas, appoint staff, perform both a sales and delivery function and get involved at grass roots or get someone else to. The one thing you cannot delegate is the responsibility for the business.

You should be involved in all decisions of significance; all of these will have elements with monetary implications. The definition of 'significant' will depend on the size of your business.

Generate options

Should you be discounting to get the sales, or paying commission to others? Unless you understand the figures it is difficult to know which is best or how to combine the two without a double whammy.

By knowing that you can apply the calculations to help you decide, there is no limit to the number of options with which you can start. They can be discounted later but you will not find yourself frustrated at a later date when you realise that you could have done things differently and achieved a better result.

Long term impact

Whether it is taking on premises or staff or buying a printer, have you thought through the ongoing costs of the purchase?

Even simple calculations on paper can help identify what costs you may be taking on. A list of associated costs can be a starting point for someone else to find out the likely figures. You need to know – not necessarily need to do.

If you are looking at purchasing a car for yourself, you are likely to decide how long you want it to last, what sort of resale value it may have, how much the car tax and insurance will be, what are the likely servicing costs. Many people go through these calculations away from the business. It is just as essential to take this approach within the business.

Sources of funding

There are many sources of finance and I don't intend listing them here. However, what I will say is stating the obvious – different sources have different types and levels of cost involved.

Do you know what percentage your credit card charges you? You may have seen on television some of the payday loans that advertise 2,000 plus percent interest per annum. If they gave an example rather than only the percentage, people would understand that if they borrow £100 they will need to repay interest of £2,000 over a year if the original sum has not been repaid. This is legal, as it is clearly stated, but do people understand the figures? You are in business and need to make sure you do. And read the small print for early settlement and penalties and other hidden costs.

I sometimes get asked 'should I lease or buy a vehicle?' It may not just come down to cost. If you have no available funds to buy outright, it may be that a hire purchase agreement would suit you. If you want to plan for a regular monthly outlay with no hidden repair costs, then a lease could be better. This is basically the same as renting with the landlord paying for the maintenance. The one clause to watch is the projected mileage. If you underestimate this you could get a very large bill. If you are looking at lease purchase remember you will need to save for, or finance, the purchase at the end of the lease agreement.

I appreciate this is not all about money, but having sufficient to implement your decision is one of the key factors. Working out the numbers may mean that, by taking a small loan for a deposit, you have enough to sign up to the interest-free on the full purchase. The interest you pay on the deposit loan is far less than you would have paid if you had chosen to finance the whole amount.

It is this sort of reviewing of options that allows you to select the best. Burying your head in the sand or taking the first deal offered is not always the best option for the business.

SUMMARY

This chapter has set out why you need to understand the accounts and figures that make them up. Whether it is to prevent fraud, enable business growth or simply to sleep well at night.

Knowledge will give you power and credibility.

2 Know where you are now

You will not be able to judge progress until you know where you are starting from. This chapter looks at what you might have now and the questions you should ask before we can rely on it as a basis to plan and measure growth going forward.

SOURCES OF HISTORIC INFORMATION

The best plans will be based on facts rather than guesses. What can you do to give yourself the best chance? Learn from history would be my answer, whether it is your history or someone else's. What I mean by this is, if you have not been in business long, others have. Whether they have been a success or a failure, there is something that can be learned in every case.

This chapter sets out some of the sources of the information available to you, and also considers its quality. Having lots of industry-specific ratios can be useful, providing you know the context. For accountants and the tax office an old and well used example was that of the traditional butcher. In a well-to-do neighbourhood, they can charge high prices for their rump and sirloin steak but may struggle to sell stewing steak and liver. In a poorer location, mince, stewing steak and liver may be the fast selling products while the steaks have to be discounted to shift them. So from one cow of the same size and quality, different butchers can expect to make different amounts of money. They may also find that their rent shows a regional difference which can add to their costs.

So, any information gathered must be taken in context and with a certain confidence in its accuracy. For this, the best information available is any historic information you have. With respect to its accuracy, this will be discussed later.

Year end accounts

If you are a limited company these are required to be produced each year and a summary of the figures submitted to Companies House. Whether or not you are a limited company, HMRC requires a copy with more detail. This is required so they know how much tax you are liable to pay.

It will still depend on the size and composition of your business as to whether an external party needs to prepare the accounts or whether you can do it yourself. Although it may appear cheaper to do them yourself, how much confidence do you have that they are correct and taking advantage of particular tax reliefs that may be available? How do you keep up to date on changes in reporting requirements? Accountants registered with a recognised body are obliged to do training each year; that is part of what you pay for.

Recently, I had a client bring in his books close to the year end. I sent him the first draft with queries and the draft tax bill. He paid this figure. By the time I had put through the final adjustments and recalculated his tax, he received £2,500 back in overpaid corporation tax, this being the difference between the first draft and final version of the accounts. This was more than double his accountancy bill. I am not trying to promote the benefits of engaging an accountant, just to say they do have their uses.

Having said this, I am not suggesting that you should leave it all to your accountant, far from it; you know your business much better than they do. It is to your benefit to record everything. It makes preparing your accounts easier and therefore should reduce your bill. With respect to recording everything, I always say it is better to record too many receipts and payments and then for the accountant to let you know some payments cannot be included as a business expense than to expect your accountant to invent payments at the end of the year. Parking is a classic example. Although it may only seem a small amount, if you feed parking meters an average £10 per week for a year, that is £500 and at least £100 extra tax that you would be paying the taxman if these payments were not recorded. If this amount doesn't matter to you, please call me and I can give you my bank details so you can give the tax saving to me! If you add a nought to the end, you can see that these sorts of things do start to add up.

Having agreed that these historical accounts will be made up for every business, the only reason you may not have them to aid your planning going forward is that you are a new business that has not yet built up a trading history. We can look at ways around this later.

For an existing business, the most recent accounts are likely to be less than twelve months old. Not only are they of interest to see how the business has performed over the years, they should give some indication as to the breakdown of figures. How much has been bought, sold and the expenses of the business. If you have not looked at them in detail before, your accountant may have come up with what he, or his computer system, feels is an appropriate breakdown for your industry. Do they allow you to look back at rates and rent separately over the last three years? How much do you pay out on delivery of goods to customers? I appreciate that important figures to you may not be of relevance to someone else, that is why the accounts need your involvement, not just your accountant's.

Later in this book I will be starting to explain the figures, but for now I ask that you start to track down the last three years' accounts, more if possible, or less if you have not been trading for that long.

Management accounts

These accounts are most often created within the organisation unless your external accountant has been specifically asked to prepare them. They may be monthly or quarterly and used to review progress and aid decision making within the organisation.

In the past you may not have prepared these. Going forward, when you have finished this book, you will understand their benefit.

If you do have your annual accounts split into shorter time periods, you will start to see that you need to bring in some money each month or quarter just to pay the running costs of the business. More particularly, they can be used to see how profitable the business is on a monthly or quarterly basis.

As with any management information, you can wait and have accurate information, for which there will be costs involved, or you can have the quick and rough figures. If you employ an accountant and competent book-keeper within your organisation, they should be preparing monthly accounts for you. By reviewing these you will be able to see how the business is doing up to the end of last month. What you are looking at can then be the basis of decisions going forward.

If you are keeping the books yourself, or have less experienced help, monthly figures are still of great benefit providing you then apply common sense to what you are looking at. A bill for the production of your annual accounts may only come in once a year, a management accountant will allow for this and may put an estimate of one twelfth in each month so that when the bill arrives, it is already included. You may choose not to include the figure monthly, but have a reminder list of annual payments at the bottom of the figures for the month. This ensures you don't forget to allow for it without the complication of having to become a management accountant.

The other benefit of having D.I.Y. accounts rather than none is that the figures are being kept up to date and reviewed on a regular basis. If you get a new standing order going out of the account, you are more likely to remember within a month of it starting rather than fifteen months later when your accountant asks you what it related to.

If the figures are not reviewed monthly it is not critical but it is good to be able to have a month-on-month comparison. To know that your stock is building up or your sales are increasing or that you are spending more on advertising than you thought, all are useful facts that can influence what you do next.

VAT quarter figures

Knowing that you will get penalties if you submit your VAT return late is a common reason that some businesses have correct figures up to at least four months ago. If you are not VAT registered you actually have more reason to keep your books up to date as you will need to register within 30 days of reaching the threshold for registration. The sales figure is calculated on a rolling year basis of total invoicing/sales. You always need to know what last month plus the previous eleven add up to. If you fail to register you will not only be liable for penalties but have to hand over 20% (at the current rate) of your takings for the period when you did not register, but should have done, even though you did not charge your customers the 20% extra. Speak to an accountant before registering as there are some special schemes or deals which may be of benefit to you. Some schemes you can only take advantage of when you first register.

For information, one of the schemes currently available allows you to pay over less VAT than you have charged your customers, but you cannot claim for VAT you have had to pay. It is known as the flat rate scheme. This can be very beneficial if you do not have to pay VAT on a lot of what you buy, such as a business working from home where the main expense is wages which are nothing to do with VAT. This method does not prevent you having to record your payments as the taxman will still need to know when calculating the tax due on the profits for the business. The benefit is that you do not need to know which and how much VAT is in the payments you make.

If your accountant works out your VAT, that's fine. What is important is that you know how they have come up with the figures so that the information you are using to run your business is as correct and complete as it can be. You don't want to plan assuming you can keep all the money from sales, when 20% needs to be paid over to the taxman as VAT plus another percentage for business tax at the end of the year.

Historic cash flow

One critical figure in any business is the cash available. However many sales you have made you cannot continue in business if you can't afford to pay the wages or buy the materials to deliver the sales. If you find you have to wait for customers to pay you before you can fulfil the sale, you may need to look closely at your figures.

Although you might pay some bills by monthly instalments, others may be due once or twice a year, such as the tax on the profits of the business. If you haven't put money away ready to pay the bill, it can be a terrible drain on resources and nervous energy.

There may be seasonal trends in the business. If you sell Christmas trees, you may have a cash inflow in December and have arranged to pay the supplier for the trees in January. Don't spend all your takings knowing there is a large supplier bill to pay. Pubs are another industry where good takings over Christmas mean good takings for the VAT man later when the industry is typically quieter.

Looking back at your payments and receipts is what I mean by historic cash flow. It might sound complex, but at its simplest it means look at your bank statements over the last year and see when you appeared to have plenty of money and when you didn't.

I have one client who would appear to be cash rich. What he is actually doing is building up a float so that if there is a business that has closed and is selling off its equipment, he has sufficient funds to bid for some items and often gets them at a fraction of the new price. This particular client is in heavy engineering and therefore the discounted price may be £100,000, so I dread to think what the new price would be. He has made great savings by having the cash ready.

Understanding when you are going to have demands on your cash is an important part of the planning process.

How reliable are your current figures?

It is good to have figures available but dangerous if you cannot rely on them. To have sales double counted or missing expenses is going to give you a misleading picture of how the business is doing.

The gut feeling of the experienced business owner is not to be ignored, but any decision should be based on fact. Whether you are trying to justify your plans to your co-directors, your bank or your staff, having facts to support your decision or to reject others adds to your credibility.

How recent is the content?

As described above, the more recent the figures are, the better information they can give you. It is easy to forget expenditure over time, especially if it has been paid in cash or personally. Checking your records when supplier statements arrive and sending your account customers statements will help ensure the completeness of the most recent records. With the ability to review bank transactions via the internet daily, there is little room for the excuse that you didn't realise the current position.

Some of these tasks, you can delegate. One of my clients who was going through a seasonal challenge with cash flow asked his internal accountant to email him each morning with not only the bank balance but the items not yet cleared and the receipts promised. The partner was then in a better position to decide which suppliers could be paid and payments authorised.

When were they last audited?

If you are looking at the reliability of the figures, I would ask the question 'when did someone outside the organisation last look at the figures?' This may have been your accountant or auditor, it may have been a business advisor or it may have been a non-executive director. Two questions arise: why were they looking at the figures and what have you done to incorporate their feedback into your records and record keeping?

The question as to why they were looking at the figures will help you understand whether checks were done and figures questioned. Some accountants just take your figures and prepare them in an acceptable format for submission to the authorities. They then ask you to sign to say you have given them all the information. I have certainly taken over and worked with clients where the 'audited' accounts have been incorrect. I don't just mean that an expense has been incorrectly described, I am thinking of a company where the notes to the accounts described a property valued at £1.2 million being included that had been sold two years before. I can only assume that the auditor had not updated their template. The same company last year had a £20,000 difference. They asked me to come and find it as their auditor couldn't. This time the auditor had included a bank account that had been closed the previous August but they had not updated their figures. At least the firm knew who to ask when their auditor couldn't resolve the issue!

It is errors such as these that confirm to me the importance of the business owner being prepared to ask questions. Even if you don't want to do the detailed work, at least know what size the numbers ought to be. If you use a calculator I am sure you do a mental check before relying on the answer. The same should be true when looking at the figures of your business.

Who prepares them?

Who prepares the figures for you? How experienced are they? This may be an unfair question as there are many different levels of figures. Recording daily taking may be a simple task, tracking who still owes you what is a little more complex and working out what work you have done and not yet invoiced for, or beer you have bought and not yet sold, may be a much more specialised task. All these tasks should be part of the figures you review.

How often are you going to be looking at them? If you know that the best you can manage for now is quarterly, that's fine. Don't pay to have monthly accounts prepared that are left sitting amongst your emails, have more accurate ones prepared quarterly and ask the accountant to go through them with you.

If you do pay to have external involvement in quarterly accounts, make sure they are presented in a way that you can understand with a breakdown of figures that are of interest to you. Remember you are the customer. If the supplier cannot provide them, move on to someone who can, even if you have to pay a little more. Buying a cheap suit that doesn't fit and lives in the wardrobe is a waste of money. The money would have been better spent towards one that fits properly and wears well. This is another example where you do things in the domestic environment but, for some reason, do not apply the same logic in business. If you do, I apologise, you are one of a small minority.

What knowledge do they have of the industry?

I have the advantage of age and the experience of working with a wide variety of industries. I therefore have a good appreciation of what factors to consider and percentages to expect when working with many clients. However, I also know my limitations. To cover this, there are industry comparisons available and even looking through trade magazines will give you a feel for factors likely to influence the figures.

When I am tax planning for clients, I always ask the questions that do not show in the books. What has happened since? What plans have you got? What other factors may affect your income over the coming years? I can then make sure I don't take a track which would lead them to a tax saving one year and a large tax bill the next.

So, to get the most from your figures, make sure you do not compare them with other industries or the same industry in other locations without considering what factors are the same, and which are different.

If you know your industry better than your accountant, be prepared to help them out. They will want to come up with the best answer for you and should be prepared to build in factors that they may not know they don't know. You can help educate your accountant.

How much knowledge do they have of accounts?

In the same way that you know your industry, so your accountant should know theirs. By all means challenge the figures they come up with, but then listen to their explanation as to why they feel the figures should be as they have presented them.

The good thing about being a business owner is that you need to understand the figures, but don't actually need to be the one to prepare them. Does the cost of bottled water include VAT? Providing someone knows the answer, it doesn't have to be you.

I am not talking about the process of book-keeping, which is the recording of the transactions. It is important that this is done correctly otherwise you can fall into the trap of rubbish in, rubbish out and HMRC do not accept ignorance as an excuse.

The important thing to know is that the person preparing the accounts understands accounts. They will be able to spot extreme examples of errors in recording. I have seen incorrect accounts that have been presented to the HMRC where the money taken out by the owner including his salary and paying for school fees has been entered as expenses of the business. This is wrong and distorts not only the profit but the tax bill and the owner's view as to how profitable the business is.

When comparing year against year, you need to have confidence in earlier years' figures as well. As with monthly versus quarterly accounts, how many years back you are going to review is up to your time, energy and trading history. If you are looking for loans, investment or to sell the business, the chances are you will need to produce at least three years' figures. I appreciate that if your business is new, you won't have this information but your aim should be to build it up.

How complete are the records?

When reviewing, particularly recent figures, are you sure everything is included? A client I saw recently had forgotten he needed to include the purchases on his business credit card. He had included the total amounts paid but had not looked at each statement to find out what had been purchased or how the money had been spent.

This can be a simple oversight but to have a lump in the accounts which is potentially unanalysed is not helpful and may actually be wrong. If you are not sure whether the payments are for fuel or goods that you have sold on, this could have a noticeable impact on the costs of goods sold and therefore on how much you need to charge to make sure you cover the costs for each sale.

THE TRACK RECORD OF YOUR BUSINESS TO DATE

One thing is for certain, your business has a track record. Even if you only started up yesterday, you have already established the date your business started. As time goes by, it will have a history which cannot be changed. The historic information will be used in a variety of ways. It is partly about reputation, so don't squander it, you may not get a second chance. Reviewing the next section will help you manage and plan for a good reputation.

If you have been established longer, you will relate to some of the sections below. I appreciate that they may not all apply to your business, but it is better to consciously exclude, than to overlook an area of potential impact.

Trends within your business

Many businesses have trends in their sales, some of which are obviously based on seasons, such as sales of Christmas trees, some are less obvious such as some restaurants' sales are linked to the paydays of their customers. Do you know what trends there are that affect your business?

As suggested above, much of this will depend on the industry you are in, it may also depend on your location. Whatever the cause, it is important that you plan to allow you to maximise your revenue during these times of higher sales opportunities. But it is just as important to plan for the slack times.

In some industries there are dates when staff are not permitted to take leave. Would this benefit your business? Are these restrictions on holidays in their contract of employment?

The title of this chapter is Know where you are now. Where are you in the month/year (or longer cycle) that your business has experienced in the past? If you are new to your business, and don't have historical figures to refer to, put your customer hat on and think what would influence you as to when in the year you might make a purchase and how long the sales cycle would take.

There are very few businesses where customer demand is static. I am struggling to think of one as it does not apply to even utilities, food, insurance... I could continue.

A good way to gather information about the trends in your business is to look back at historic figures. How they have been recorded will dictate how easy the information is to access. But like many facts, if you don't ask the question you cannot know the answer.

If you find this level of information is not currently available, consider how it could be extracted from your current records. Everyone has to record them for, and be able to prove their figures to, the taxman so why don't you get there first and use the information for your benefit rather than waiting for an investigation by the taxman?

Below are some areas to consider; how they might have historically impacted on your business, and might in the future. Although some are from an academic perspective, I have included them because I believe they are relevant to understanding how your business is influenced by the wider picture.

Industry sector performance

How do you compare to others in the industry? This information is available although you might find that you have to pay for it. Some inexpensive sources include trade journals, trade associations and other industry specific bodies.

If there is legislation or other requirements that affect the industry these can be detailed and superimposed on your figures to see whether you have been following or bucking the trend.

One quick note is that you need to make sure you are not comparing oranges with apples. Some businesses may invoice at the start of a job, others at the end, so if you were to compare month-on-month sales against a competitor, you need to take this into account.

Some accountants charge once the accounts are completed and submitted to the taxman. Some accountants sell their time and knowledge on a fixed fee basis with payments being made monthly over twelve months. With these monthly payments, you can see that this would hide peaks and troughs and address the feast or famine situation in the case of cash. However, if you are looking at resources to complete the work, you still need to know when the workload peaks will occur. In the case of my training and coaching services, I charge before the work is undertaken.

When comparing yourself to your competitors, remember to ask what they do that is the same, what they do differently and why they might do things differently.

Your availability

Looking back since you started the business, what impact has your availability, or that of other staff, had on sales? How many sales have you lost because you were too busy to follow up? How many sales have you lost because you were chasing the few weak leads you had rather than looking for those more likely to buy from you?

Although this factor is not based on money, the resulting level of sales can be. By reviewing these sorts of statistics, even in general terms if you haven't got facts to support your assumptions, you can start to identify what may be relevant in moving your business forward.

Although some of the points raised above may be more appropriate to a sales and marketing book, when you are looking at the figures and how to take the business forward it is critical to know the broader 'why' rather than just looking at the results. If you know that business has been lost because you have been too busy, what could you do to streamline the process so your time can be better spent and therefore more sales made? This is not a time management book - perhaps that will be the subject of another book I write!

Political

Have there been any strong views that have been expressed which may have impacted on your customers' thinking, or ability to spend? Changes in law are in a different section, much of this can be attitude and opportunity.

A recent example was the changes to opportunities for those installing solar panels. Overnight the government announced a change which affected much of the industry, leading to a sudden rise in sales to customers wanting to beat the deadlines, followed by a dip when the incentives were withdrawn, or at least reduced.

Another example of political influence on customers is the duty on alcohol or fuel and the impact on sales as a result. Have you ever queued at a petrol station before the fuel increased in price following an announcement in the budget?

Economic

Have there been particularly high or low interest rates? What have been the levels of employment and job security? These factors can both influence personal and business customers.

Socio-demographic

Have you got an ageing or transient population that you serve? If you run a nursery, or are a childminder, but there are few young families moving into the area, how long will you be able to find customers?

If your customers historically lived and worked locally, but now are commuters with cars, how will this affect your business?

Consider what is sold in national supermarkets. There are some store locations where you can buy fresh chicken mince, others where shark meat is for sale, others will sell veal. The stock available will depend on what local customers want to buy, not what the supermarket has available to sell.

Technology

This area is one that is very relevant to both the customers' demands and the method of delivery. How many shops had an online presence ten years ago? Taking and placing orders using the internet has made a difference to both expectations and the ability to process and communicate. However, if technology fails, this can damage the reputation of the business as well as the ability to deliver. If Amazon refuses to advertise your product for a month, this can result in a drop in sales and, in the longer term, lost customers.

Legal

There is usually some warning given of any legal changes that could affect your business, but it depends how far in advance you are planning as to how greatly they can take you by surprise.

It is key that you keep up to date in your industry. If they introduce laws about qualifications to perform particular tasks, do you have enough qualified people to do them? Will you lose business while you train them up?

If you look at your trading history, have there been changes that have impacted on the way you do business? Changes in legislation may also have increased or reduced the number of competitors. The deregulation of the postal service is one that immediately comes to mind.

Environmental

There are many factors that can affect a business and cause peaks and troughs. The important thing is to recognise them to ensure that you can maintain and potentially grow the business.

How is your business affected by the weather, the month, the tax year, school holidays? There is a long list of possibilities, but you know your business so I will leave the extension of this list to you.

Lending requirements

One good reason to review the history of your business is to know projected borrowing requirements. I had one client who bought in goods from China. One third of the cost had to be paid with the order, one third at the start of manufacture and the final third before they were put on the boat. Approximately another quarter of the value had to be paid by way of VAT and import duty when the goods reached the UK. They were then transported to the warehouse where they sat until shipped to the customer, who had a policy of penalties for late deliveries. So the customer needed the goods to sit in the warehouse, rather than not being readily available and then delivered late. This, of course, incurred warehousing costs. Several customers had also negotiated 90 day payment terms, with one customer getting 120 days. This trail of demands for money before getting any from the customer meant my client needed to fund the sale for over six months. This was one cost that was not fully calculated and therefore brought into their pricing. The company could not sustain this and is no longer trading.

Although this seems an extreme example, this is why builders will tend to ask for staged payments. It allows them to buy the bricks and mortar and pay the wages while the house is being built. This has also led to some builders offering discounts if you purchase 'off plan' so that they have money before they start the work. The chances are that you are a cheaper form of finance, through discount on the final price, than paying interest to the banks. It may also be that you are an easier catch, with fewer hoops to jump through than are involved when borrowing from the bank. At least the builder has a definite customer, unlike the bank's view that a customer will still need to be found once the house is complete.

The above examples relate to bigger projects, for smaller projects or service-based industries, the issues can still be the same. In accountancy, it is who pays the wages of the staff doing the work until the job is complete – and then how long does the client take to pay? This is why many accountants now prefer to charge on a fixed fee basis with monthly instalments.

When looking at your business, it is important to appreciate when the cash needs to flow out and when it will flow in: more of that in a later chapter.

IDENTIFY WHAT YOU SELL

Are there any obvious groups of products or services that your business offers? For me it can be broadly split into accountancy, training and coaching. If I choose to, I can then split accountancy further into tax, accounts and payroll. The advantage of doing this is to see what resources are used in the delivery of each area and to work out what benefit you get from each and then decide whether they are worth continuing with. You may also decide how you may need to market different areas in different ways, if you do not already do so.

How should you analyse your sales for greatest benefit?

I am often asked how people should split their sales for analysis purposes. For me, there are two overriding factors. What are you going to do with the figures when you have got them? And how practical is it to obtain the figures?

Sometimes, when people go into business, they have read books and understand the benefit of a detailed breakdown of the turnover/sales figures. If you have signed up to a franchise that dictates exactly what and how you can sell your products, they may want a detailed breakdown as they have other outlets to compare. In this situation there is little you can change by way of promoting one line or dropping another. If you run a pub with food and rooms, it is useful to know how much of your profits are non-drink sales as this might have a smaller percentage of costs attached. As you have the facilities anyway, this area may be worth promoting if it is not operating at full capacity. If the rooms are already full, do you need to spend more on advertising?

As referred to above, the other important factor is how easy the figures are to collate. For the pub, the till has a code that can split the takings across the types of sales. You could even ask it to tell you how many of what type of meals you sold – or could you? If someone asks for chicken curry with chips, yet the standard is rice, how do you tell the till? How much does it matter? This appears more of a question for marketing, but you can then review whether you ought to charge a different amount, since chips cost more than rice.

Coming back to the main question of this section, what do you actually currently supply to your customer?

To whom do you sell?

This is key within any business. Know your customer. Although this is often viewed as more marketing focused, it is important that the costs relating to your sort of customer are recognised.

A simple example of the range of customers for one industry would be those firms who deliver to large customers who accept one order a month via a courier, and those whose customers expect a small delivery several times a week.

What follows are a few questions that you should consider. Although we are looking at costs and profitability, the expectations you have of these will have an effect on the costs involved.

What do they expect?

How would you categorise your best customers? Are they individuals looking for a bargain or looking for a quality product or looking for a personal service? You could be selling the same product/service and fulfil all of the above. The important question is, what is your customer's perception?

If they want a no-frills service it does not mean they want a poor quality of service. It does mean that they are not expecting extras unless they pay for them. The current example of this is the no-frills airline where the passenger flight price is only a small proportion of the total price after paying for food, luggage, booking costs, tickets etc. Even amongst these budget carriers, some have a better reputation than others and this confirms it is not about price.

The reason this is important will become more apparent when you consider pricing. For now, just review how you would define what your best customers expect.

The reason I say your best customers is that I am presuming you want more of the good ones and fewer of the bad. By bad I mean the slow payers, those who are never satisfied and take up a disproportionate amount of time for the amount they pay.

How would you categorise them?

Are your main customers business or consumer? This is a common split and the answer may well be both. If this is the case, do they expect to be treated differently? A business customer will often expect to set up an account and not pay for 30 days; a consumer will expect to pay for the goods in advance or on receipt. As I explained earlier, this can have a major affect on the funding of your business.

Marketing is something I am trying not to cover in this book, but the funding of marketing cannot be avoided. If you sell through agents, they expect some form of commission, if you are selling via the internet you will find both Google Adwords and PayPal want their slice of the same sale.

If you have just sighed because everything today seems to refer to the internet, I apologise. I could just as easily have referred to passersby or those with already booked appointments who enter your physical premises for which you pay rent and other running costs. Many banks will charge you to pay in cash. This is another cost which is often forgotten with face-to-face sales.

All the time we are starting to recognise the costs associated with sales. The intention is that by understanding each element and how many there are, you can better understand what is involved when considering pricing. Knowing where you are now provides you with a starting point to move forward from.

Are you a substitute?

Do your customers have a preferred supplier who is available to them? How can you make yourself the preferred supplier? Looking at this can certainly put a different perspective on how you view your customers and what you offer them.

Service or product?

Are you providing a service or a product? I would suggest that nowadays there is a very fine dividing line between the two.

When I provide a training course it has a start, a finish and content in the middle. I could define this as a product of the training course or the service of educating someone. Does it really matter?

The dictionary defines a product as something that is made to be sold, usually something that is produced by an industrial process or, less commonly, something that is grown or obtained through farming. When I looked up service, I was given a broad choice, but in this context I suppose I mean 'the act of dealing with a customer'. As the 'dealing with' is undefined I would suggest that this does cover what I intend. The big thing for me is that customers are involved in the service and therefore it is more volatile, depending on the customers' needs and expectations.

Bespoke or standard/cost of customisation

So your customers know what they want, but is it what you offer? Can they have a product or service off the shelf or do you need to work with them to specify, design and build your offering to match their requirement?

If the customer is having something made to measure, they will need to recognise they have to pay for this specialised individual service. How much effort do you have to put in to working with the prospect to understand and possibly document their needs? It is often this stage that is missed when businesses are looking at how much to charge. Because this stage often happens before they have agreed to buy from you, the time is often written off. If instead they were to buy a standard 'one' without reference to you, how much of your time would that free up?

When reviewing where you are now, consider how many one-off changes you are making as it may be that some of these can be incorporated into another 'product' that could be sold but without further effort being put in on the supplier's part. At worst, consider what you could re-use rather than starting from scratch – even if it is just the format of the proposal.

UNDERSTAND HOW OTHERS SEE YOU

When it comes to finance, other people's perceptions are as important as yours. With most people, they won't spend money unless they are confident you can deliver what you are offering. Although you may offer a guarantee, how much use is it if you are not there to claim against if the need arises? As I get older and wiser, I am not necessarily becoming more suspicious, just more cautious.

When we moved into our current house in 2000, we had double glazing installed with a ten year guarantee. After eighteen months the seal had collapsed around the front door and our daughter's window didn't open properly. We called the company to find they were no longer in business but, interestingly, the phone number went through to another double glazing company who told us the old one had now closed down. To be fair to the new company, they did come out and fix the door seal but they would not fix the window. It later turned out it had been wrongly fitted. I wonder if that is why the old business was no longer operating.

If I was to move house and have double glazing fitted again, I would first consider whether I wanted a guarantee that offered me more than the levels offered by the Sale of Goods Act that I would have had to enforce using trading standards or, at worst, the courts. I would put a value on the guarantee and use this to influence my choice, rather than just making sure that a guarantee was provided.

For larger contracts for my companies, I will look at websites, check with Companies House and occasionally download the accounts to understand how long they have existed, been trading and who the directors actually are. I can find out even more about the company.

In the same way you may do this for some of your suppliers, remember that prospects may well do this to find out more about you.

Banks

The advantage that banks have is that they can see your bank balance with them. This can lead them to draw wrong conclusions as they are only looking at part of the picture.

I have one client who has over £150,000 in his second business account and the bank gets very upset. The truth is that he wants to be ready to purchase large capital items when they come up at auction and to pay for these he does not want to start transferring funds from longer term deposits where he would lose interest by making a short notice withdrawal. He knows he loses interest, although currently not much. By having the cash on standby, he has taken advantage of this almost hidden opportunity.

He might be rare in being cash rich, but anyone looking at his historic accounts would see a pretty healthy, growing company. If you can build up a pot of cash, think how much you could save on interest payments. In fact, by having planned borrowing and repayments made on time, you are building up a credit history for your business which is a positive.

Overdraft

The banks often make a fixed charge called an arrangement fee to allow you to borrow their money by way of an overdraft. This fee may be charged each year for the bank to review your requirements even if there is no change in what you need or in the level they will allow. An overdraft is basically a loan of varying amount with a maximum limit and no set repayment dates. The banks may well insist that it is secured against personal guarantees by the directors. In the case of a sole trader business, you are personally liable anyway.

If the use of your overdraft is seasonal, the banks will be able to see this. If you are regularly up to your overdraft limit – and exceeding it, the banks may well be in touch.

Staying within your agreed limit – which may be nil – is a good way for the bank to guess how carefully you are watching your funds. This can be very time consuming for you if funds are tight whereas the computer at the bank will no doubt tell them instantly if you exceed your limit.

Loans

Loans are a common way of funding expenditure for the business. However, make sure that you keep up the repayments and make them on time.

As we all know, late or missing payments are one of the fastest ways to damage your credit rating. This can not only affect your opportunity for future loans, but whether suppliers will offer credit facilities and the trust customers have that any deposits they hand over will be used towards delivering their purchase, not paying off the debts of the business.

There are many types of loans. I have listed the heading under Banks but suggest you view it as applying to all lending companies, including hire purchase and mortgage companies.

If you trade as a limited company and need a loan, try to get the loan for the company rather than using your personal cards, or a personal loan. It is very difficult to get the interest paid for by the company and therefore be allowed to reduce your tax bill. If the loan is in the company name, there is no problem.

Other facilities

There are other types of facilities offered by the bank such as invoice finance. This is where the banks will give you a percentage of the cash from sales up front. See Borrowing under Where does the cash come from in the next chapter for a further explanation.

Suppliers

Do your suppliers view you as a good customer? One way to find out is to ask them. Other ways to judge are to review how likely they are to give you advance warning of information that might be of benefit. This could be changes in the sector that may affect your business, deals they have coming up or how they deal with any queries you have.

I can think of one of my suppliers for whom I am a small customer by way of turnover, but we work on a give and take basis. I give him as much notice as possible of what I need and he knows that I am happy to be fitted in around other larger clients. However, when I have an emergency, he will also work out of hours or pick up the phone and talk to me to see how we can jointly progress the resolution as fast as possible. And yes, I do pay him on time!

Your reliability

The main area that suppliers will look at is whether you pay on time and are you happy with the service or product they provide.

When your business places an order, your supplier should be confident that: there is authority to do so; the order is unlikely to change; someone will be in to take receipt of the delivery; they will get paid on time and if additional items or services are later requested, you will accept the extra cost without dispute.

If you re-read the last paragraph, is this how you would like your customers to treat you? What goes around comes around!

Level of service

What level of service do you provide as a customer? This may seem a strange question, but having thought about how others might see you and the factors that make a good customer for them may help you to identify three factors. The first being what you expect from your customers – you can test if this is what you supply as a customer to your suppliers. If a delivery arrives within your organisation, how is it acknowledged and passed to the correct person? By seeing how your organisation acts, you may be able to identify what can be done to make your life easier for your customers. Argos currently phones approximately an hour before a home delivery. As a customer, I can then ensure I am available and ready to take collection. This benefits me and reduces the need for rescheduling deliveries for them: win-win, the ideal situation.

The second is how do customers know what to expect from you? The third is how do you communicate what level of service they should expect? If you order a meal to be delivered to your home, and they say it will take an hour, you don't get on the phone until the hour is up and the food has not arrived. If they work towards a forty minute actual delivery time they shouldn't get many phone calls. It is all about setting customer expectations and exceeding them.

Customers

Many customers will take their lead from how you treat them. If you are sloppy and don't care about customer satisfaction, why should they care about you? If you are smart, accurate and efficient, it is not unreasonable to expect your customers to reflect this approach. A simple example is if you chase any outstanding payments from customers as soon as they become overdue, the customers will get into the habit of paying on time. If you let the account drift and don't chase up, some customers will become slow payers as they would rather have the money in their account than yours.

Flexibility

Having said that, some customers will try to take advantage and others may want to negotiate. How would you feel if a customer asked for the discounted price on a high volume purchase but then wanted it split over several deliveries? If the multiple orders had been placed for the same volume it would have cost them the higher price. At first glance, you might say if they are prepared to pay up front, you are happy as you have a larger committed order. You will have multiple costs for delivery though, so how much extra is it costing you? This comes back to understanding your figures. If you understand the cost of delivery, you can make a decision about whether to accept the order. You know the cost of chasing debts and if you know whether they are good payers or not, this can again influence your judgement.

Would your customers see you as a flexible supplier or do they simply buy 'off the shelf' with no options? Are there options you could offer which are actually at no cost to you?

Reputation

This can take some while to gain, but can be easily lost. Word gets about within an industry so make sure that each customer is treated with respect and leave them in a place where they want to recommend you.

You could have a reputation for charging people for interest or admin fees on late payments. If prospects complain you can point out what your terms and conditions are and suggest if they pay on time, it will never affect them. It is a bit like a speeding fine, if you stay within the speed limit you won't get points on your licence for speeding.

As this book is primarily about finance, I won't spend time on all aspects of reputation but my final point relates to refunds and guarantees. How small is your small print? Have you ever had to act on guarantees? When considering costs, it is one more cost that needs to be included if you offer them. You may also have a refund policy. What do you do with goods that are returned damaged? Most firms have an element of wastage, but consider what causes this cost to your organisation. Have you built it in to the average cost of sale?

Credit Companies

Whether you are looking to purchase on credit or whether it is potential customers or suppliers checking you out, the view of credit companies can be critical.

There are many factors that affect your company's credit score, including how much cash you have in the bank, whether you have had credit before, whether your business has any County Court Judgements (CCJs) against it. The better you can keep your books and pay your suppliers on time, the better your financial reputation will be.

How do you compare to competitors?

Some industries are known to be poor with money; others are thought to be good. Some sectors are heavily regulated, such as solicitors and, I was about to say, the banking sector. The fact is they are regulated, but sometimes organisations do not comply so, although an assumption can be made, there is always the exception to prove the rule.

In the same way, some businesses need money tied up in equipment and stock, while others, such as consultants, can operate a very lean business as their stock (of knowledge) is held in their heads and does not show on paper and cost money to store.

What is your industry standard?

When comparing yourself to others you should know what your industry standard is and should have some idea as to what factors cause the variations. In the pub industry, beer may be a 50% mark up, but wine and lemonade are considerably more. If you sell food in a pub, you may expect to have more wine sales than a drinkers' pub that does not sell food.

This is one example that most of us can relate to, but you should know your own industry. To date, the information may have been available but perhaps you did not understand or appreciate it and how you compared. By the time you complete this book, it should all become clear and you can work towards being the best in the industry and where others would like to be. As with any goal, you need to understand what you are trying to achieve and how to get there, so keep reading and you will find you can make a difference.

Who are your competitors?

Once you start looking at your competitors, you will start to understand the niches within the industry. If you are going after the same customers to fulfil the same need as another business, then the chances are they are a competitor.

Having established who your competitors are, you will need to see what you can find out about them and their finances. This might be through their ex-customers that you have taken on, publicly available figures or shareholder reports. Alternatively, it could be from their marketing material or quotes that prospects or customers have shared with you.

Make sure when doing comparisons that you are comparing like with like. The time taken to do product deliveries within Yorkshire or Cornwall may be different from Hertfordshire, where the county is smaller and there are simply more roads per square mile.

What makes you different?

How would you sum up what makes you different from your competitors? It may be that you own the premises you work from while others rent. It may be that you manufacture rather than having to buy in products and can be more flexible in your production or delivery times.

I suggest you list these factors as some may help with sales conversations, others may help you understand why some competitors seem to be making more money than you.

If your list seems short, you may need to do some research to make sure you do know. What seems obvious to your customer may not be apparent to you, as you are too close to your business. Alternatively, you may neglect to list something obvious to you which may not be known to your customers because you have never told them. You could always try asking your customers why they chose you.

What do HMRC think?

Her Majesty's Revenue and Customs have a huge amount of data they can use for comparison which they have built up over many years.

In days gone by, their inspectors were issued with tables of percentages for different trades in different locations. They could then judge how close you were to the standard and then you could discuss with them if you felt you were justified in being different to the norm.

With the use of computers, all figures are collected and compared much more quickly. A simple example is when you submit your VAT return, using the HMRC website, the system will let you know if the 'figures do not seem correct'. At this stage, it is only checking simple maths, but once it has captured each quarter's figures for each type of industry, you can understand the volume of data to which they have access in order to make comparisons.

As a registered business, whether you have a £4,000 or £4 million turnover, HMRC will be watching you!

YOU NEED TO CREATE A BASELINE

A baseline is a known starting point. If you are going to be monitoring your figures and seeing growth and controlling costs, you will need to understand where you are starting from.

'I want to grow my turnover by 10% this year' is a worthy statement, but what is your current turnover? How much profit do you make from it? If you increase sales, what costs are also going to need to increase? Have you got the capacity to cope with an extra 10% or is major investment in staff or equipment going to be needed? Understanding the figures will help you prepare for this growth.

Going forward, know how you are doing

If we carry on with the goal of increasing sales by 10%, is this planned as a steady growth through the year? Maybe you are taking on an extra sales person in month three who will generate the extra sales from month five to the end of the year and beyond. At what point will you measure how they are doing? It is all very well for your sales staff to document how many new contacts they have made, how far down the sales process they are with each, but what also matters is how much has actually been invoiced and paid for as a result of their efforts. Are the sales team paying for themselves by way of increased sales and profits? Are they covering their costs and more? Unless you know where you started from, you will not know how far you have come.

The other benefit to knowing where you are starting from is that you can create a plan and monitor what actually happens against the plan. Is where you are now where you want to be? Unless you know where you are, you won't know whether you need to make changes and, if so, to what. If you understand what your baseline is you will have a better idea of what, if anything, needs changing. Even if you think nothing needs changing you still need to monitor whether you are achieving the 'no change' situation.

What things are measured

I have not yet specified what needs to be included in a baseline but by gathering information that you find of use, you will have a good idea what needs to be measured going forward. I referred to the number of leads and conversions, although these do not appear to be financial figures, they contribute to working out the acquisition cost of a customer, i.e. how many leads you need to make each sale. To start on the exercise of deciding where you are now, you will start to highlight information that you do not currently collate but could be useful as part of your planning process.

There is a management saying 'if it can't be measured, it can't be monitored'. Most things can be measured in some way but before you go mad taking it to extremes, you will need to consider how much effort is involved in gathering the information against how much benefit you can get from the results. You also need to consider what factors control the results and whether they are under your control.

There may be some measurements that you want to make in future but the data is not there to create a baseline. Don't waste too much energy going back, but decide how to collect the information going forward. The fact you are considering these is progress in itself.

SUMMARY

You should now know where you can find your historic figures and how reliable they are likely to be. When considering business growth, you need to know where you are starting from.

Don't assume that everything will remain static. Many factors can influence both sales and availability of resources. By looking at historic figures you will start to see what affects your business.

You should consider what you are selling, to whom and how it is being delivered as all these will affect costs and customer expectations.

So far I have not asked you to do any calculations or figure work. Hopefully you are starting to understand how many factors can impact on both historic accounts and your plans for the future. This appreciation of the factors involved is more important than being able to use a calculator. I can hear a sigh of relief!

3 Reviewing your accounts

When you get a call from your accountant telling you the accounts are ready for signing, how closely do you look at your accounts, how many questions do you ask?

If you have monthly or quarterly figures prepared, who do you sit down with to understand what the figures really mean to your business?

What follows is a list of typical headings, what they mean and what they might include. There are also some questions you might like to ask. Not all items are relevant to your accounts, but by going through each, it might help you understand other sets of business accounts as well as yours.

Some of the later sections only apply to limited companies, but I have indicated where this is the case.

TRADING AND PROFIT AND LOSS ACCOUNT

This is a report covering a period which can be a year, a quarter, a month or whatever is of benefit. The title should always state what period is covered. When using this report for review, it will be useful to have a second column of figures for comparison purposes. These may be the same period last year. There is nothing to stop you having multiple columns being the last twelve months being shown a month to a column.

As with all reports, decide what media you prefer. Whether it is paper that you can draw on, or on-screen where you may be able to easily access more information, the choice is yours.

Turnover

This should be the sales you have made in the period, excluding VAT and any discounts that you have given. It is the headline figure that most people look at when discussing the size of the business.

It may have been adjusted for work done but not yet invoiced at the end of the year. There would also be an adjustment at the start of the year for work invoiced at the beginning of the year that was completed in the last financial year. Ideally this figure for work in progress would be supplied by you to your accountant. Alternatively they may have looked closely at invoices after the end of the year and created their own figure.

If you sell products the same may apply where goods have been delivered to your customer so are no longer in stock, but the invoice was not raised until after the year end date. An adjustment should be made for this.

Many people use the word 'sales' when they really mean

turnover. That is fine if you appreciate that there is a slight difference. Technically, sales is just one element of the turnover. Many business owners will include VAT when talking about 'sales' as they view it as the money coming into the business.

When looking at the growth of a business, turnover is typically the figure that is monitored year on year. If you start to review it on a more frequent basis, consider any seasonal fluctuations, bank holidays and other factors which would give rise to variations.

Cost of sales

This is a section that may not be present in your accounts if you are supplying a service. It is the costs associated directly with the items being sold.

Sometimes this heading is used in the service industry where staff are recharged or subcontractors used. There is a direct relationship between the sales and the employment of the staff whose time is sold. There may also be other costs as part of the sale, such as providing them with pensions, training etc. without which they could not have their time sold to particular clients.

Where goods, rather than services, are being sold, the following headings may appear as a subset of this major heading.

Opening stock

This is the stock purchased last year which has been available for sale this year. It may, or may not have been sold during this year. The fact that it was available to be sold is why it is included in the accounts.

It should be valued at whichever is the lower of 'cost or net realisable value'. This means either the amount it cost you, or, if it is getting old such as last season's colours or fashion, the amount you might expect to get for it if you were lucky.

The idea of this method of valuation is that it is as close to realistic as can easily be calculated.

In practice, a formal stock take is still done by many industries with coloured stickers (or a similar indicator) being put on each box included. By using different colours each quarter or year, it also gives you an idea of how quickly stock is moving.

With computerisation, many firms rely on their records of sales and purchases to decide what stock they should have. Note the word 'should', they also need to find out what they actually have. With damages, theft, free samples and exchanges being given, the best computerised systems are not always 100% accurate.

How do you prepare the figure you give to your accountant, for stock, at the end of the year?

Purchases

This is the cost of items you have bought for resale to customers. It may be that you do something to the purchase before the customer receives it, such as turning fabric into suits, or you may have purchased it in the same form as the customer receives it, such as a hardback book.

As with sales this will be after discounts and VAT have been deducted.

Where there are foreign currencies involved, giving rise to exchange differences, these are dealt with later as they are a consequence of when the purchase was made rather than directly relating to the purchase of the item for the sale itself.

Closing stock

At the end of the period there will be some stock which has

not yet been sold to customers. As it has not yet been sold, it needs to be taken out of the costs. The valuation is as for opening stock described above. It should not include items sold that have not yet been despatched.

This should be the same figure that appears in the balance sheet as it is what the business has, by way of goods, on the last day of the period being reported upon.

Carriage in and import duty

Where goods are being delivered to your premises, there may be an element of carriage that directly relates to purchases as described above. If this is the case, it is sometimes rolled into the purchases figure but you may want to identify the costs of getting goods to you.

If you are having multiple small deliveries, how much is this costing you versus the cost of storage of fewer but much larger deliveries? Is there an issue with the shelf life of the product that forces you into this position? A single barrel of beer delivered to a pub can attract a delivery fee of £50 in addition to its purchase price of say £90; weekly deliveries may be free. Is it really worth it?

Another cost which is often forgotten when sales prices are calculated is the import duty being paid when the goods reach the shores if they are purchased from overseas. The amount of duty will depend on the type of goods being imported. If the cost of freight and say 3% import duty are omitted when the costs are being worked out to give a sales price, any sale of these items could actually result in making a loss on the sale.

Direct labour

This is the cost of staff to produce whatever it is you sell. These may be the people who provide the service or manufacture the goods.

Labour will also appear further on in this chapter, but under this heading it is the staff that are directly involved in the goods you sell or service you provide.

Depending on the industry, the valuation of closing stock may include an element of labour. If this is the case, this heading would appear before closing stock. This is more common in the manufacturing sector.

Other direct costs

This may be the cost of vans for service engineers if your business supplies field engineers as its main line of business. Another example would be the cost of insurance where your primary business is the transport of antique furniture and pictures and the customers are offered the option of insurance for a particular trip. You then pay for the insurance on an individual policy basis linked to individual sales.

Yet another example is subcontractors in the building industry. They are not staff as they account for their own tax and national insurance and purely send in a bill for hours worked to the business using their services. In order to monitor this type of payment there is a whole system run by HMRC known as CIS (Construction Industry Scheme).

As there is such a wide range of 'others', I will stop here in the hope that you appreciate the general rule that this type of expense would not happen if the sale had not taken place.

Expenses

These are the other amounts a business pays out during the year to keep the business running. They can be grouped in a way that makes most sense to you, but for tax returns they will need to be grouped into categories identified by the tax office.

For smaller limited companies, the expenses are usually grouped into: employee; premises; general; legal and professional; interest payable.

For sole traders there are specific headings that need to be completed on the tax return. I will use those on the 2012 tax return to explain what types of expenses may form part of your accounts. On the tax return there is also a column to allow you to exclude items that you cannot claim against tax, such as speeding fines or penalties for late submission of tax forms. These do need to be included in the accounts as they have been paid by the business and therefore affect the profit.

Wages, salaries and other staff costs

If you are a limited company you will need to keep a separate note of the directors' salaries and benefits. If you are a sole trader, you may choose to include a salary for yourself but when presenting the figures to the tax office, this will be excluded as you will be assessed (taxed) on the profits the business has made, not on how much money you have taken out of the business.

Salaries and wages of staff should include the amount you have to pay for employer's national insurance. Although the staff do not get paid this amount it is payable as a direct result of you employing them. In reviewing the wages bill it is worth ensuring that employees are getting paid at least the minimum wage. If they are being paid piece work, i.e. paid according to output, they must still be paid what equates to the minimum hourly rate across the week.

If you are looking at figures on a monthly basis, consider holiday pay and bonuses. These may be paid in single additional amounts and may need to be 'evened out' across the year when looking at profitability per month, or planned for when considering cash flow.

Other staff costs will include pension contributions and health insurance if you provide these for your staff. Another group of expenses is training courses. These may be to keep your staff legal, such as first aid refreshers, or developmental, such as conflict resolution or team leading. Finance for non finance managers is an area of training often neglected. Do you provide it as part of your development for managers? If you don't, I know a good trainer ...

Car, van and travel expenses

This can be further broken down depending on whether it is simply mileage claims that you or your staff make, or if the business provides vehicles.

If vehicles are owned or leased, then you may wish to split the expenses further between tax and insurance, repairs and servicing, fuel and lease costs. Remember, once a vehicle gets older it may require more work and money to keep it on the road. Also the bigger the vehicle, the more fuel it will use.

A business may have a fuel card for convenience but it may be worth checking how much you pay for your fuel every so often and see if convenience outweighs the special deals some garages might have.

If you lease vehicles remember to keep an eye on the mileage as the penalties for exceeding the annual allowance can be very expensive.

If your business is paying for public transport, what is your policy? Can staff travel first class, or fly business class or do you expect them to take the most economic method of transport? How often do you check?

I am often asked whether a business owner should buy or

lease a car. The first point to note is that if you are a director, or it is for staff, there will be a taxable benefit. This means a predefined figure will be added to your salary and tax due on the extra 'income'. Although this is typically collected through your tax code, this is dependent on whoever does your payroll remembering to tell the tax office.

The advantage of leasing is that you know how much the vehicle will cost you each month and, dependent on the small print, a substitute vehicle may be provided if yours is out of action. You will need to estimate the mileage you expect to do to ensure you are paying the correct tariff. If you are doing 30,000 miles a year, the lease company will have to provide more tyres and services than if you only do 5,000 miles a year. There is often a minimum term so again, ask the question so you can make an informed decision.

If you purchase a car, it does mean that it is yours at the end and, if you want to change it or dispose of it, you have the freedom to do so providing any finance is cleared. Although you can claim VAT for the purchase of a van, assuming you are VAT registered, you cannot claim the VAT when you buy a car, unless it is the tool of your trade, such as a taxi.

Rent, rates, power and insurance costs

This is group of costs that can seriously distort comparisons between similar businesses.

If you own premises, you will not have rent to pay but you may have a loan and therefore interest on the loan to buy the property. Repairs to maintain the building will come under a different heading.

Rent for serviced offices may include power and rates so there would be no figure available to include under these headings. An owned property would have these headings, as would rented premises if you are responsible for your own utilities.

Where rent is paid quarterly, you may want to make adjustments when looking at monthly figures so that it does not appear that no rent is paid two months in three. This again highlights the importance of knowing at which report you are looking. If it is a cash flow report, the cash will go out one month in three, if it is accounts, the profit per month will be taking account of that month's rent only.

There are different types of insurance. Under this main heading the insurance is for the building and the contents. Other kinds of insurance that would be included in the accounts, but possibly under different headings, include: public liability, product liability, professional indemnity, employer's liability, goods in transit. Your business may not need all these, but if you are not sure, I would suggest you check.

One question I would ask is how efficiently you are you using your space? If it is to store papers that you do not need regular access to, could this be done more cheaply in a storage facility? If you have too much space, are you allowed to sublet?

Cleaning is another heading you may feel is appropriate as part of the premises costs. It could also come under office expenses if it is only the office that you pay to have cleaned.

Repairs and renewals of property and equipment

Repairs do not include major renovations but are the payments that you would count as maintenance to keep the thing functional, whatever the 'thing' may be.

This would therefore include service contracts and warranties which are basically a way of evening out any repairs that you might need.

Renewals is a little more difficult to define. Some of this

would depend on the type and size of your business. When I am teaching book-keeping, the general rule I suggest applying is 'will it last more than a year?' If it will, it may well need to be treated as a fixed asset – see below. Not only will the taxman treat it differently, but you should too as the money you spend on 'it' this year will give you multiple years of benefit.

If the item is small, it may be difficult to keep track of it over the years, and it may have no real resale value, a waste bin being a typical example. So, the level at which an item would be counted as small will start to depend on the size of the business. If you are a pub with bedrooms, using a washing machine at least twice every day to wash sheets and towels used by your guests, you might hope it will last more than a year, but if it packs up you would scrap it and buy another. However, if you did not have bedrooms to rent out, you might use it once every two days to wash staff polo shirts or a few tea towels and the expectation would be different, so it would be counted as a fixed asset. This is why it is not always easy to know which heading to put things under.

As an accountant, I will ask my client if I am not sure how they will use these types of purchases. Not all accountants do, but perhaps they should. You will expect them to justify their decision to the taxman so it is up to you to make sure they have sufficient information to make the decision.

Phone, fax, stationery and other office costs

This is one heading I would definitely split into several as, if not controlled, the various costs can increase without you noticing, especially if it is not you recording the transactions.

Phone

Even the heading of 'phone' immediately begs the question of mobiles versus landlines, line rental or telephony system versus call costs. As always, it will depend on the size of the business as to what level of headings you need and are of use. However, taking a careful look at some bills may cause you to check that you are on the most cost effective tariff. As your requirements change, so you need to monitor what is best for you. If you have phone contracts, ask if each person has sufficient free minutes since the extra minutes can be very expensive.

This is where the business owner should use the art of delegation. With many phone providers they will do the analysis, you just need to put in the request. If you have had any known extremes, remember to ask them to build this into the review.

With package deals it is not always possible to split down to the level you would like. A best guess may sometimes be necessary.

If you use an answer service you may choose to have a separate heading. As always it will be what makes sense and would be beneficial to your business.

Fax and internet

The fax might be part of your computer software if you have one at all, or you may have a dedicated line and machine. As with all headings it will be what best suits your needs for the business. What benefit will you get from separating the cost?

In the same way that the fax may be part of the phone bill, so might internet connections. You may want to monitor these, particularly if you have mobile access by way of a dongle. Technology changes and so do the costs associated with each method of internet connection. Do not presume that something that was the best for the organisation last year, will also be the best for the next five years.

Stationery

Should printer cartridges go under stationery or printing? For most businesses classifying them as stationery is fine. We never used to put typewriter ribbons in a different category and they did the same job.

If you are doing a lot of printing, for example manuals for a course, you may want to use a separate printing heading for these. This is because it suits the needs of the business since you may want to consider outsourcing this in future. Do you realise how much the toner costs? If it is separated you will start to be aware of some of the hidden costs. Paper and binders for manuals are often identified, but the cost of the printing isn't.

Printing

This may include printing of advertising and marketing material. If it is purely the odd price list flyer, you may well decide to include it with stationery and the printing of general correspondence.

Postage

Again this may or may not be relevant to your business. If it is of no interest, don't waste time in separating it. If you are doing marketing by post rather than email, there may well be good reason to monitor costs.

If you are shipping goods via the post then this may be a material figure and does need recording, otherwise it can become a hidden cost that bruises your profits as it does increase with your turnover.

Information and publications

In some industries there is a need for text books or other reference materials. If appropriate, make a heading and use it. If not, don't waste your time and effort.

Subscriptions and licences

If your business has subscriptions to a variety of trade organisations you may not be aware of the total cost over the year. They seem a good idea at the time but do you actually make the most of your subscriptions?

Often licences are a legal requirement so you need to have them, but are they appropriate and is the data on the original application still valid? Looking at the figures will raise the questions, maybe you have someone else who can find out the answers.

When looking at the accounts, you may decide to apportion the cost across the period it covers. This is particularly true of a multi-year licence, as paying this year will also give you the benefit for the next two years if it is a three-year licence. This type of adjustment is known as a prepayment – see below.

Computer costs

This can include software and similar payments to allow the computers to operate for the benefit of the business. In my case this includes hosting software for large files that I send to my clients.

Computer servicing could be deemed to go here or under repairs and renewals. I re-iterate my point that it would depend on the business. The important thing is being consistent.

Sundry or miscellaneous costs

These should be kept to a minimum. Firstly, because the taxman might think you are hiding things under this general heading and secondly, for your own benefit. If there are lots of the same sorts of payment put under this heading, shouldn't they have a heading of their own? How are you going to monitor them if they are lost in a bigger figure?

This heading could instead appear later in 'other business expenses'.

Advertising and business entertainment costs

Nowadays this is often a broad heading with subdivisions for different types of marketing activities.

As with renewals, you may need to consider whether some things are long term and if the cost should be spread over several years. An example of this would be the initial outlay on a website. The monthly hosting and updating may well be current marketing, but the upfront cost may need to be spread. This would be done by analysing it as a fixed asset (see balance sheet) and a percentage payment shown each year.

If you are reviewing monthly accounts, make sure that where a single payment has been made for advertising in a monthly magazine for twelve months, the cost has also been split across the twelve months. It is this type of apportioning that can be viewed as a hassle but will make the accounts more accurate. This is important when they are being used to make decisions.

Advertising and marketing is an expense that can be compounded if not monitored. It is worth reviewing what types of expenditure you have had in the past and what plans you have for the future to help you decide on headings and how far the figures need to be broken down. Although budgets and financial planning are not covered in this book, marketing is something where you might plan to have a small floating allocation to be used on 'too good to miss' opportunities. But be clear about the criteria as to when it can be spent and what benefits you expect to gain as a result. Targeted marketing can be a very good investment.

HMRC has very clear rules about what is acceptable entertainment and therefore what is allowable for tax purposes. I do not intend going into these except to say it is sometimes a little worse than just not being allowable against profits. It may be that they are counted as a benefit for the person receiving them and the employee then gets a tax bill as though they had been awarded extra salary. The best advice I can give is that you consult an accountant for advice.

Interest on bank and other loans

Whether you are a sole trader or a company, it is interesting to know how much you spend on interest as a cost of borrowing money. This can arise from a bank overdraft, paid as part of a hire purchase contract, or simply as part of the monthly payment of a bank loan.

In a small business it is often tempting to pay for things privately on your credit card and have the business pay you back over a period of time – or when it can afford to. The down side of this is that the expense sometimes gets left out of the accounts. The interest that you as an individual pay can be difficult to prove as a business expense as it may be mixed with personal payments on the card. An expense claim you then put through the business would be very difficult to get approved by HMRC, especially if you are the director of a limited company.

There are different methods of calculating interest allocation for hire purchase agreements and similar fixed payments across the life of the agreement. This is because at the start of the loan you owe most of the capital and therefore a high amount of your repayments are only interest. By the time you get near the end of the agreement, most of the sum borrowed has been paid back so not much interest is due. It is basically viewed in a similar way to a repayment mortgage.

A question I am asked is should you have a loan or an overdraft? This will depend on how quickly you expect to pay back the borrowing, what rate of interest you will be charged and what the arrangement fees are. The important thing about a loan is that you will be repaying it, rather than having an overdraft that can just sit there for years on end earning the bank lots of your money in interest and arrangement fees.

Bank, credit card and other financial charges

These are all the other bank charges such as arrangement fees, credit card processing, cost of withdrawing or banking of cash, processing cheques to name a few.

Like all costs, this should be monitored to make sure you are getting a good deal from your providers. You may have had twelve months' free banking at the start, but how much do you pay now?

If your business uses PayPal or a similar provider, there are typically different rates depending on usage, so don't presume that the rate you had at the start still applies.

Yet again, it will depend on the business as to how much analysis you may find useful. If most of your customers pay by credit card, how much are you paying out as a percentage of sales to collect the money on each order? If your customers pay by cheque, how much does your bank charge you to process a cheque? Is this the same amount as the profit on the sale?

Irrecoverable debts written off

The hope is that you do not have any bad debts.

I have discussed earlier some of the options for collecting money so that it does not reach this stage. However, sometimes it does happen and when it does it eats into your profits. Thankfully you don't have to hand over the VAT. Or if you have to, you can claim it back.

In some industries there is an expectation that x per cent of sales each year will not be paid for. This heading should be used for those that have actually gone bad and will never be paid, not the provision for those that might. As the annual accounts are often prepared several months after the year end, someone should have a good idea whether the outstanding amounts are likely to be paid or not.

Potential bad debts are dealt with differently and are referred to within Trade Debtors in the Balance Sheet section of this chapter.

Accountancy, legal and other professional fees

This is another heading that may well deserve subdivision. Too often I see different suppliers of services all collected under one heading. If you are reviewing where your money has been spent, it is useful to know whether it is on professional services that you do not need every year, such as engaging an employment specialist to assist in staff contracts.

Consultancy

Some years you may seek professional advice, and some years you might not. If you have a human resources issue, and do not have a specialist team internally, you would be well advised to seek help. The cost would be included under this heading.

Another example of professional help coming under this heading is Health and Safety. Depending on your size, you may feel it is appropriate to get a professional in to do your risk assessment or advise on a particular issue.

Book-keeping

If you have an external book-keeper, you may want to separate this cost from an external accountant. This may help you keep a check on expenditure so you can see at what point a part-time or full-time member of staff may be more cost effective than outsourcing.

If your existing administration employees provide this service within their job roles, there would be no need to separate it. This comes back to my point that the headings you use should be those of benefit to you and your understanding of how your costs are split.

Accountancy

This is a classic example of when costs need to be adjusted to the relevant year. The amount you pay the accountant for the year's work regarding the annual accounts is not known until the work has been done after the end of the year, unless you have taken on a fixed fee contract with no extras. The way this is dealt with is that a provision is put in being the estimate of the accountancy bill for the year end work. At the start of the following year this is reversed, so that when the bill is paid it cancels out last year's estimate, allowing this year's estimate to be entered as the relevant figure.

If you are getting external help with monthly accounts, you might also choose to separate this so it can be monitored. Remember, if you don't measure it, you can't monitor it.

Auditor

Some companies require an audit which is an independent review of the figures for the year. This is most common when a company matches certain criteria as set out by the Companies Act. One of the criteria is turnover. Once this reaches a certain level as specified in the Companies Act, you must appoint external auditors to prepare the accounts and 'check up on the figures'.

If your turnover is below the limit you do not need to appoint an auditor unless you are in certain industries, your trade body requires one, or your shareholders or lenders or franchisor insist on one.

You may also be in a position that if you have bought a company, the old owner may be entitled to a percentage of profits/sales in the early years. The small print may refer to an audit to make sure they are getting what they are due. It is worth checking who can perform this audit as I had one client who was in this position. The old owners were, in fact, happy that an external accountant prepared the accounts although the solicitor had included the words 'audited accounts' in the sale contract.

Legal fees

Whether you have a boundary dispute or are getting help chasing bad debts or defending a claim, there may be times when you engage a solicitor.

As this type of expenditure can be sporadic and is often not planned, it is well worth separating these costs.

Let's hope that the only time you need to engage a solicitor is when you are expanding and looking to acquire another business, larger premises, to sell the business or similar positive situations.

Depreciation and loss/profit on sale of assets

In simple terms this is the difference between what you initially spent on equipment, furniture, cars or other long term items and what they are worth now.

Depreciation

I usually describe this as the wear and tear reduction in value for the year. The rates used will depend on expected life, but it is common to group them into bands so you may have some items at 15% and some at 25%. The external accountant will usually make a best guess depending on what you have bought in the year. The method and percentage does not usually change over the time you own the item.

They are not the same definitions the tax office use as they have their own methods which can change from one year to the next. These are known as capital allowances.

There are two methods of calculating depreciation. They are known as the straight line method and reducing balance method.

Straight line calculation

Straight line is when the item has a limited or fixed life and it would be reasonable to say that it decreased in value the same amount each year.

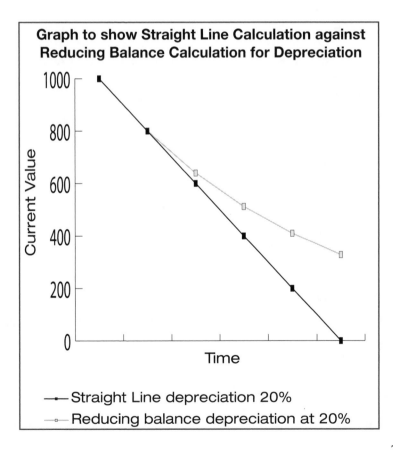

This method of calculation is sometimes used for computers where their useful life may be estimated at four years and therefore a quarter of the cost is included in the accounts each year. They will have nil worth at the end of the four years.

Reducing balance calculation

This is where the percentage is applied to what is left so as to reduce by a much faster rate in early years and to acknowledge that there is some value even when it is old. A typical example of this is a car which loses value as soon as you drive out of the showroom, but as it gets older the drop in value reduces and even if it is a heap with no MOT, it has a scrap value.

Profit/loss on sale

This is the difference between how you have adjusted the value down from the original purchase price and the amount you actually get when you sell or scrap the asset. If it is stolen, then you would use the insurance proceeds as a 'sale price'.

The purpose of this entry is to compensate for under and over allowances in earlier years.

You do not do a calculation for wear and tear (depreciation) in the year of sale as it will be rolled up into this figure.

Amortisation

This is the same as depreciation, except for things you can't touch such as goodwill, leases, patents etc. It represents their decrease in value.

The classic and easiest example of this is a ten year lease which each year decreases in value (in simple terms) by one tenth each year. At the end of year ten it has no value.

Other business expenses

This heading is designed for anything you feel does not fit any of the headings above. An example that immediately comes to mind is donations.

The headings you have under this category will depend on what is of use to you. It is not uncommon to have a heading labelled Sundry Expenses or Miscellaneous which is fine, providing everything that you are not sure about does not get dumped in the category in the hope it will be forgotten about.

Beware, HMRC may ask for a breakdown as to what is in here so make sure it does not get used to hide suspect payments made by the business.

Suspense or Not Known

This should never appear in the final accounts but can be useful if you need to 'park' a payment or receipt somewhere until someone can offer advice on where it should really be put. With some computer software, you may have to move an amount here before moving the amount elsewhere, as the system will not let you do a direct transfer. That is fine, providing there is nothing left in this account when you review the accounts for the last time.

Other income

This is the non trading income of the business. It needs separating for the tax computation, but more importantly, you as a business owner should be looking to separate income not resulting from your main business.

This heading will not include gains on sales of long term items as they would be included above under profit on sale. The original item was purchased for the benefit of the business, so the sale should also be categorised as such.

The only exception to this would be when part of the company has been sold off as a lump, i.e. the business has been split. Because this is not part of the usual trade, it would be shown under this heading.

Other items not included are insurance claims. They would be included in the cost of repairs or replacement. If the claim is for loss of earnings, this would be related to usual trade and should be included higher up this report.

Below are some common types of other income.

Interest received

This is most commonly the bank interest received on a deposit account. It may also be interest received from long outstanding debts on which you have charged interest as opposed to a penalty. Yet, as often happens there are fine dividing lines between how income and expenditure are classified.

Rent received

If you are in a position where you sublet part of your premises, this is an add-on to your main trade or profession and should therefore be shown separately. It may be that since you rent your premises anyway and the value is so small, you would rather treat it as a reduction of the rent, rather than additional income.

Like many types of expenditure, the big question is how material is it? For management and review purposes you may want to keep it separate so you do not fool yourself as to how much rent you are actually paying.

If your business owns the building and rents out the flat above the shop, it should be shown separately as it is another source of income for the business and is not the primary purpose of the business.

Dividends received

If the business owns shares in another business, it may well be receiving dividends. As income they must be included, but they are not why the firm is in business, i.e. its primary trade. The income from dividends would be included as other income.

Corporation tax

This is the amount of tax due to be paid to HMRC in relation to the company's profits each year. The profit figure is calculated in a different way by the tax office so will not be a straightforward percentage of the accounts profit in most cases.

Dividends proposed and paid

This is only relevant to limited companies. This is the amount of profit it has been decided to distribute to shareholders in the year or period. It is in recognition of the investment they have made in the business.

Not all profits will be distributed as the company may choose to retain some to build the business.

Dividends can only be paid where there are profits to share and may be done quarterly, half yearly or annually. They may be referred to as interim dividends if they are paid out during the year. They will be termed final dividends if they are the last for the financial year. Under the Companies Act the accounts must distinguish between those actually paid out and those proposed but not yet paid.

Trading and Profit and Loss Account
For the year to 31st December 2013

		2013		2012	
		£	£	£	£
Turnover			560,333		510,236
Cost of Sales					
	Opening stock	12,000		10,340	
	Purchases	224,000		198,112	
		236,000		208,452	
	Less: closing stock	14,000		12,000	
		222,000		196,452	
	Carriage and import duty	5,000		4,300	
	Direct labour	20,234		17,564	
	Other direct costs	15,000		12,000	
			262,234		230,316
Gross profit			298,099		279,920
Expenses					
	Wages, salaries and other staff costs	60,123		58,123	
	Car, van and travel expenses	23,654		20,334	
	Repairs and renewals of property and equipment	5,678		6,987	
	Phone, fax stationery and other office costs	3,214		2,911	
	Advertising and business entertainment costs	5,667		13,932	
	Interest on bank and other loans	999		1,276	
	Bank, credit card and other financial charges	345		431	
	Irrecoverable debts written off	240		0	
	Accountancy, legal and other professional fees	4,632		4,298	
	Depreciation and loss/profit on sale of assets	2,250		2,250	
	Other business expenses	300		345	
			107,102		110,887
Net trading profit			190,997		169,033
Other income					
	Interest received	45		34	
	Rent received	12,000		12,000	
	Dividends received from investments	230		123	
			12,275		12,157
Net profit			178,722		156,876
Corporation tax payable			36,194		35,300
			142,528		121,576

Note: Dividends paid (for limited companies only) are usually shown by way of a note rather than being shown after corporation tax as they are a distribution by choice rather than a cost to the business

Balance sheet

This is a statement of what the business has and owes on a particular date. Unlike the profit and loss account which is for a period from and to, the balance sheet is always described as being 'as at' a particular date. It is a snap shot of the state of the business.

If you apply for a personal loan or an independent financial advisor wants to do a fact find, they will ask you your income and outgoings per month (similar to the profit and loss account) and how much you own, such as a house and how much you owe, such as the mortgage, credit cards etc. This is equivalent to a personal balance sheet.

If you owe more than you have, it is a cause for concern. It does not mean that you have to give up, just that you and others will be cautious. As a home owner, if you are in negative equity (your mortgage is greater than the current value of your house) it is not a problem unless you want to move. As long as you keep paying the mortgage, everyone is happy. You may find that you cannot get further finance, but as long as you satisfy your existing debts no-one will bother you. The same is true in business.

A business, particularly in its early days, may owe more than it owns. The most common scenario is where the directors have personally funded the start-up of the business and do not expect repayment for a couple of years, until the business can afford to pay them back. The important thing when looking at the figures is that the business is generating income and will be able to pay them back.

Even if the business has been going for some years and still not made a profit, there may be other businesses which would be prepared to take it on as you have done a lot of the groundwork. If your business is in this position, don't just close it and give up without consulting professional insolvency and business recovery specialists who may be able to help you realise some cash rather than none.

Whether it is you or others who are looking at the current position of the business, it is the balance sheet that they will review first.

If you are a limited company of any size, the balance sheet is public information and can be obtained by anyone by paying Companies House a nominal fee. As such, I believe it is important that you understand the elements of it so you can understand others' balance sheets as well as your own.

Fixed assets

This is the value of major items which have been purchased with the intention that they will be around for more than a year. They may have been purchased using a mortgage, loan or hire purchase scheme. They are actually owned by the business and any papers such as car registration documents or deeds of property are in the name of the business. Any loans against them will appear further down the report.

Intangible

These are typically listed first and, in simple terms, are things you can't touch.

As years go by, their value will decrease. This reduction is done by way of amortisation (which has been described previously, towards the bottom of the profit and loss section).

Leases and patents

Leases and patents are one group of purchases that will come under this heading. The lease may be granted on a property that the business occupies. The patent may be the key to your business and what you produce. It is not your registration of a patent, but the purchase to allow you to use it.

Goodwill

Another example of an intangible asset is goodwill. This typically arises where a business has bought another business and, as part of the purchase price paid, an element for the good trading history and reputation. In a small business, this can arise when a sole trader business becomes a limited company and carries on with the same customers, providing the same services, using the same suppliers and it is only the legal entity that has changed. An accountant would be involved in working out what value to put on this and how it needs to be treated from a tax viewpoint.

Tangible

These are large purchases that you can touch and see, unlike the intangible items.

They have been purchased to allow the business to carry out its primary purpose. If this is not the case, for example a work of fine art, it would appear under investments rather than here. Also, if you deal in cars, the vehicles waiting to be sold would not appear under this heading, but under stock as a current asset – a continually changing amount.

Land and buildings

To some extent this is self explanatory. Actually, it is a little more complicated due to tax rules. The fixtures and fittings would not be included in here although they often are for ease with a small business. But once the numbers get bigger, there are companies who specialise in splitting the value of a building between the bricks and mortar and the fittings, such as sockets, air conditioning and other 'optional' things.

This is one example of where it can pay to employ professional help as the numbers get bigger. Even the accountants will employ specialists if they feel it is appropriate.

As tax rules change from one year to another, I would not suggest whether you should rent or buy without knowing more facts. If you purchase the property, should it be as the company, the directors or the pension scheme? My plea, as always, is to ask advice, discuss the options and consider the numbers before you commit to anything. In a situation such as a property purchase, please seek help from an accountant who is also involved with tax before signing anything. There are even VAT implications in property purchase that can influence the decisions and cost you thousands if you find out later what you could have done. A solicitor can help with the purchase but you can't expect them to advise on VAT, company and personal tax implications as well. There are currently changes to how business premises valuations are split between building and fixtures (see below) which solicitors cannot be expected to calculate.

Over time, buildings can increase in value if they are kept in good repair. It is possible to revalue them, but there are other implications so it is something that needs thought and consultation before a revaluation appears in the accounts.

Plant and equipment

This can cover a breadth of equipment that your business uses. It can be anything from a simple laptop through lathes to complete manufacturing systems. The important factors are that the items are used in the business to help generate its profit.

It is recognised that, unlike land, plant and equipment will typically decrease in value so depreciation is used as a method of recognising this decrease. This is further described in the Profit and Loss Account section above.

Fixtures and fittings

As described within Land and buildings, this can be a sensitive area. If you have display boards fitted in a shop, or whiteboards fitted in offices, these would come under this heading. They may just sit there but their presence helps the business generate profit. I appreciate a whiteboard may be only a small expense, but they do come in large sizes, and if you have multiple meeting rooms and offices to fit out, it could be a large bill. Typically, these do not wear out as fast as equipment but they will decrease in value and this needs to be recognised.

Vehicles

If you trade as a sole trader, you may well have a car or van within the accounts. You can get the business to pay all the running costs, fuel etc. but there will be an end of year adjustment for the amount of private use which is then added back to reduce the amount you actually claim.

If the business is a limited company, there is no reason that it should not own vehicles but it is important that they are treated correctly for the directors and staff that use them. HMRC will treat the provision of a vehicle as a benefit and therefore liable to tax. The amount of tax will depend on the list price and CO_2 emissions. I had one new client who did not realise this and was taxed as though she had an extra £10,000 a year income. The fact was she was leasing a quality Jaguar. As she was the only employee, she could not claim it was a pool car and available for all employees to use. The other test for a pool car is that no employee has private use and it is not taken home at night or used for private purposes. If all you need is a cheap, economic runabout, or you do a lot of business miles that would considerably reduce the value of your personal car, then it may be worth considering letting the company purchase the vehicle. The message of this book is that if you understand the numbers you can make informed decisions.

Although VAT cannot be claimed on the purchase of a car unless the car is the business, such as a taxi, other tax allowances can be claimed but there are restrictions as to how much you can claim each year. Don't assume that you can just offset the purchase price to reduce the profits in the year you buy it. It does not work like that.

Vans and lorries have different rules from cars, so it is worth seeking clarification and guidance in this situation. The HMRC's website would be one place to start.

Investments

These are items purchased by the business but are not related to its main trade or profession.

It may be something as simple as a work of fine art that is displayed at the head office and may be sold in years to come.

Another more usual example is the shares held in another business. A further example is a property purchased with the intention of renting it out when being a letting agent and a landlord is not the primary business.

Current assets

These are 'things' the business has which are, or could technically easily be turned into, cash.

Unlike fixed assets where their value does not vary, current assets may be changing every minute. Where they appear in the report known as the balance sheet, it is important to remember that this is only a snapshot. If a set of accounts show that the business was owed a considerable amount, that may have been the case on the last day of the period, but the next morning the customers might have paid. This will not show in the accounts unless they are drawn up again the next day. However, it would not be usual to prepare a balance sheet every day.

From the viewpoint of managing the business, it is some of the reports behind the numbers in this section, and the next, which you would be well advised to look at on a very regular basis.

As with many of the reports, you don't have to prepare them yourself just know what the numbers mean and what implications you should draw from them.

Stocks and work in progress

This is the value of the stock of goods that is held by the business that it intends selling to its customers or work it has done for them but not yet invoiced for.

Stock is technically valued at whichever is the lower figure cost or what you could get for it. This later method helps recognise slow moving or obsolete stock.

As the figure for stock represents things you have bought but not yet sold, it can distort the profit if not correct. I have been asked 'what should the stock be?' Stock should take the form of a physical stock take at the end of each year. With computerised sales recording, this happens far less than it used to. Computerised records do not form an opinion on damaged or missing stock. This is often only found at a physical stock take. If this has not been done, an educated guess may be the only option. An accountant may be able to confirm whether your guess sounds reasonable.

If you cannot face checking all your stock, would it be practical to do a section per month? This is not ideal but much better than doing nothing and leaving it for your accountant to make up a figure that sounds right to him.

At the end of the day, the responsibility falls on you as a business owner. If you have slow moving stock, how much does it cost you to store it? Would you be better giving it away than continuing to pay storage? Although this seems an extreme comment, I have had clients who contacted clearance firms to get rid of old stock as they could then save themselves the storage costs. It worked for them.

As an accountant, I have work in progress being time-chargeable to the client but not yet billed. Typically a business in the construction industry can be in the same position. Certain jobs are in progress across the year end. That is fine, you just need to ensure that the amount that was included as work in progress in the earlier year is not also counted as invoiced sales in the current year. This question regarding what has been included in which year's sales is a matter of clarity to ensure there is no double counting.

Trade debtors

This is the amount that customers owe you.

A single figure does not indicate if there are any amounts which are old and unlikely to be recovered, so there is sometimes an extra line for provisional bad debts. If there is a chance that not all customers will pay up, this adjustment will need to be made to ensure the accounts are giving an accurate figure. The provision may be based on a couple of specific unpaid bills or a percentage of the total. The method chosen will tend to depend on what industry sector you sell into.

When reviewing your accounts, it is very useful to also look at a breakdown of this figure commonly known as an Aged Debt Analysis or an Accounts Receivable report. This should list each customer who owes you money. At its best it will also break all debts down by age so you are able to see those that are not yet due, those that are overdue, and those that are very overdue.

It will depend on the size and your day-to-day involvement in the business as to whether you or someone else reviews this supplementary report, but someone should. If you have customers who are not paying, you might want to consider not supplying them further until they have brought their payments up to date.

Other debtors

This is the amount that you are owed from individuals or businesses, but not as a result of your sales during the year.

This may be because the business has lent someone or another business money in the short term and expect to get it back. Again, an example of this is where the director has taken more from the business than he/she should have done by way of salary and dividends they have been allocated. The result is that technically they owe the business the excess of the money. Beware if you find yourself in this position as currently, depending on the size of the 'loan', HMRC will insist that you are taxed heavily on what would otherwise be an interest free loan. They view the loan as a tax free benefit as you are not being charged interest on the loan you have taken from the company.

Another example may be deposits paid by you when moving into rented property. Although you cannot have the money back until you move on, it is your money, held by others.

It is important to know what anything under this heading relates to. It is not uncommon for it to be small amounts with no fixed date for repayment such as an advance against wages. If this is the case, you can't assume it will be paid in 30 days. I suggest you find out what the true position is. Has the employee actually left? I have seen that happen with a client I took over from another accountant.

Prepayments

These are amounts you have paid but not yet had the benefit from. A common example is where you pay your insurance as an annual premium two months before the end of the accounting year. Because the payment is time apportioned, ten twelfths of the payment relates to next year. It is therefore a prepayment towards next year's usage.

Another example is quarterly rent paid in advance. If you are only one month into the quarter, two months relates to next year, an adjustment by way of a prepayment must be made. Or, you have a year's worth of monthly advertising, but you only paid three months ago, so nine months relate to next year.

Although in many cases you could not get your money back if you stopped the agreement on the day the balance sheet is dated, it would be unreasonable and inaccurate if this year's figure included amounts which are actually related to next year.

Cash at bank and in-hand

This is straightforward. It means how much is in the bank after adjusting for cheques written, not yet cleared and bankings not yet credited to the accounts. It also includes the amount in the till and the petty cash tin.

The bank element is easy to identify, the cash you may need to remember to check.

Current liabilities

In simple terms, amounts you owe that are due to be paid within twelve months. You may have agreements in place as to a repayment date, but the small print may say 'unless we ask for our money sooner'. You will often see that bank overdrafts have this sort of clause in the small print. Others may also have a clause somewhere.

Loans and overdrawn bank accounts

The overdrawn bank account is straight forward, the loans not so.

The balance showing under the overdrawn heading is the overdraft after adjusting for banking not yet showing on the bank statement and cheques drawn that have not cleared as the payee has not yet presented them, or because cheques take several days to clear.

The total figure may also include credit card and charge card balances, so as with all summary figures, it is important to know what is grouped within a single figure. As a business owner, you should be aware of the limit of your overdraft. You may find that when you opened the account, you were required to personally guarantee it. If there was more than one partner or director at the start, each one may have been asked to sign the form. How often do you read the small print? I have had a situation where a director resigned and when the remaining director wanted to extend the overdraft, it was made clear that the ex-director was still a guarantor. Although he was no longer a director, it was a personal guarantee that the banks had asked him to sign. If you do have a change in key personnel, make sure that the banks are notified and all paperwork updated.

The loans are not as straightforward as the bank balance. For hire purchase type loans which have an agreed amount of interest to pay over the term of the agreement, the balance at any point in time will include the full amount of interest. With bank loans, there may be fixed interest known at the start, but the option to pay off early and not pay all the interest. In this case only some of the interest should be shown as owing. There are different methods of working out this interest, if the loan is large, it may be worth finding out how this has been calculated so that if you wanted to repay the balance of the loan, you know how much it would cost you. Some loans may be charged as you go at a variable rate of interest dependent on the bank rate. With these you can only really plan on the basis of best guess and you won't know what the bank base rate will do.

The other peculiarity about loans is on limited company annual accounts. Any loan where some of the balance is due to be paid more than twelve months from the balance sheet date is not all shown here, but the relevant part has to be moved to a section for two to five years. And if it is longer than that, the relevant part is moved to long term liabilities. This is as much a nuisance for the accountant trying to split the figure as the business owner wondering how much they owe. However, for the investor or interested party, it is very relevant to how much the business needs to repay in twelve months, up to five years and longer. Management accounts do not need to show this split and often list each loan agreement so decisions can be made on future lending requirements.

Trade creditors

These are simply amounts you owe your suppliers.

It may include disputed amounts, but it should show the full amounts including VAT.

As with trade debtors, you, as a business owner, should have a good feel for the size of the amounts you owe, and whether your organisation is paying on time, or surviving by not paying bills when they are due. The challenge with this approach can be that suppliers refuse to supply you ('put you on stop', as it is known) and prevent you fulfilling obligations to customers. Your customers then don't pay you on time and this can start a downward spiral.

If you are having difficulty paying your suppliers, please speak to them rather than just hiding. They are as interested in helping you pay them as you are in continuing your business.

Other creditors

Accruals

These are amounts you owe but have not yet had the bill for. A typical example is the electricity where you have consumed the power but the bill is not due until after the time the accounts are dated. A figure is therefore calculated to give a more accurate picture of exactly how much you owe.

As discussed under the Accountancy heading in the profit and loss account, this is another example of an accrual. In this case the work was not even started at the date of the accounts, but their preparation forms part of the document for that year.

Refundable deposits

Although you may have received money from customers, if they could have their money back, technically it is not yours and you therefore owe it to them up until the point at which it is no longer refundable. This is different from guarantees where the cost of putting things right or refunding the money is a cost which could happen after the sale has been made.

Directors' loan and current accounts

This will only appear if the entity is a limited company. For all other types, movements would appear under capital – see below.

A director's loan account has little movement; a current account may have a continually changing balance. The two are often combined in accounts of a smaller business. Usually the loan account has a balance equal to the initial investment, and possibly further injections of money and dividends not actually paid out.

When starting, or even running, a business there may be times when the business has insufficient funds to either pay its bills, or pay the amounts owed to the directors. As a result, the company may have an IOU to the directors which it will pay at some point in the future. If this amount is then fixed, it might be separated into a loan account for reporting purposes.

It is possible for the directors to have an agreed rate of interest with the company but the interest received in the hands of the director is counted as taxable income, so many smaller businesses do not bother with the calculation. However, as the business gets larger, it may be that it is cheaper for the company to pay the directors interest than take out a commercial loan to repay the directors. It may also be that obtaining a loan may be difficult.

It is not uncommon to do a paper transfer for mileage claimed or other amounts paid by the director. These then sit as a company IOU until it repays the director. These sorts of smaller items, rather than big chunks of cash, tend to sit in the current account rather than the loan account if both are used.

Social security and other taxes

These are the amounts you owe HMRC for VAT, PAYE and National Insurance as a business. Income based taxes are explained further in the next chapter, but in simple terms, the figure here is the tax and national insurance you have deducted from staff, or are obliged to pay as a result of paying staff or subcontractors, but have not yet handed over to the taxman.

The VAT will be the difference between what you have charged when raising invoices less those amounts you have paid and can claim for. As there are special schemes and calculations, the figure is not always this simple.

Corporation tax

If your business is a company, it will be liable to tax in its own right in the form of corporation tax. If you trade as a sole trader, or a partnership, the profits will be added to any other income you have as an individual and you will personally be responsible for the tax so it will not show in the accounts.

The calculation for corporation tax is based on taxable profits. These will be the profits in the accounts after adjusting for things not allowed to be claimed against tax, such as late submission penalties to Companies House and parking tickets, and a different calculation for depreciation (see above).

Net current assets

This is simply the current assets less current liabilities. Ideally it should be a positive number so that the amount of money you have coming in during the near future is more than you expect to be paying out.

You may now understand why loan repayments over one year should be excluded from this part of the report.

Long term liabilities

Deferred tax

This is the difference between allowances you have been able to claim and the tax bill arising if you were to cease trading and sold your fixed assets at the balance sheet date. It is the sort of figure that accountants calculate and include if it is material (big enough to worry about).

As you intend continuing in business, you can almost ignore this figure as it is to do with the tax calculations.

Loans and creditors 2-5 years

So that any reader of the accounts is clear about when the company needs to settle its debts, parts of the loans or creditors with long term agreements would appear under this section.

Many hire purchase agreements should have part of their outstanding balance appearing here.

From a management viewpoint, the total indebtedness is the most important figure, but from a cash flow perspective, knowing you don't have to find the money yet can also be useful.

When presenting limited company accounts to shareholders, tax offices and Companies House, this split is required. Sole trader and partnership accounts do not usually show this breakdown.

Loans over five years

This will cover mortgages and longer term loans. The same rules apply for the two to five year loans, in that the total amount outstanding is split across the different time periods.

It depends on who is expected to read the accounts as to what further information might be included within this section. Notes to the accounts will typically expand on this.

Capital and reserves

This section will vary considerably depending on whether the accounts are for a limited company or a sole trader, partnership or limited liability partnership.

Balance sheet
As at 31st December 2013

	2013		2012	
	£	£	£	£
Fixed assets				
Intangible		5,000		6,000
Tangible		15,750		18,000
Investments		15,000		15,000
		35,750		39,000
Current assets				
Stocks and work in progress	14,000		12,000	
Trade debtors	22,456		19,765	
Other debtors	2,500		2,500	
Prepayments	345		276	
Cash at bank and in hand	22,987		19,453	
	62,288		53,994	
Current liabilities				
Loans and overdrawn bank accounts	2,300		2,300	
Trade creditors	12,700		10,560	
Other creditors	2,000		1,000	
Social security and other taxes	6,988		5,422	
Corporation tax	26,098		22,901	
	50,086		42,183	
Net current assets		12,202		11,811
Total assets less current liabilities		47,952		50,811
Long term liabilities				
Deferred tax	1,200		1,500	
Loans and creditors 2 to 5 years	10,000		10,000	
Loans over 5 years	0		2,500	
		11,200		14,000
Net assets		36,752		36,811
Capital and reserves				
Called up share capital		10		10
Share premium		2,000		0
Revaluation reserve		12,000		12,000
Profit and loss account		22,742		24,801
Shareholders' funds		36,752		36,811

Note: Sole trader and partnership balance sheets would not have a corporation tax line. Everything under Capital and Reserves would be replaced by capital account(s) either in detail here or with the detail in a note showing brought forward balance, money introduced, money drawn and profit.

Capital account

This will not appear for a limited company. For other types of entity the detail may be here, or form part of the notes.

You would usually expect to see the amount brought forward for the year or period. This is the amount the owner has invested in the business at the start of the period.

To this would be added any monies introduced into the business and another line for amounts withdrawn.

The final entry would be the profit for the period as this is due back to the business owner. Whether they choose to withdraw it or leave it invested in the business is a matter for them.

If it is a partnership, there would be this type of movement for each partner, although if it is a husband and wife partnership, it is not uncommon for the two to be combined.

There may be other headings such as partner's salary. This is simply another way that has been chosen to split the profit. It does not go through payroll and will simply be added back to the share of profit when the tax calculation is done.

For management accounts, the partners' salaries are included as an expense of the business as someone would need to be paid a regular salary if the partner was not there to do the work. This comes back to knowing why, and for whom, the accounts are being prepared so that they provide an accurate picture.

Share capital

There may be more than one type of share capital issued by a company, but in most cases there are Ordinary Shares only.

These shares represent the ownership of the company and may be held by people or businesses.

Typically, as recognition for the investment in the company, the shareholders will be paid a dividend several times a year. The amount and frequency will depend on the success of the business as it can only pay dividends out of profits.

Share premium account

If the shares have been purchased from the company at a price above face value, the difference would be recorded in the Share Premium Account.

Anyone buying shares in the company can only get the money back by selling the shares or getting their percentage holding of the value of the company if it is closed down.

Revaluation reserve

As discussed within fixed assets, it is sometimes appropriate to revalue property. As no money has actually been gained by this revaluation, the figure is put under this heading so that it is clear it is only a paper increase in value and that money has not had to be paid out to acquire its higher value.

Profit and loss account

This will have a running balance of profit to date, less tax and dividends paid. It is therefore the net amount left in the business to enable it to carry on.

In start-up years, this is sometimes negative as costs in the early years have been met by loans and the business doesn't yet have any value of its own. This is fine, providing the situation does not continue for an extended period.

Accountant/Auditor's report

For management accounts there is no need to have this. It is simply a statement to say that someone external has produced the accounts and they believe them to be correctly produced on the basis of what has been presented.

The audit report carries a little more weight as an audit indicates that the figures have actually been checked rather than taken at face value.

There are certain criteria for when an audit is required. In addition, certain professional bodies may require one, or a majority of shareholders can insist on one. The firm providing the audit will be appointed with the consent of the shareholders and it is one of the items that forms part of the Annual General Meeting. As this book is to do with figures, I am not getting sidetracked into company secretarial and administration matters here. That would be another book which I do not intend to write (although I have run courses on it).

Depending on the type of accountant you use, they may well do a certain number of checks even for an accountant's report as they want to make sure you have given them the correct figures. Not that they don't trust you, they just know that errors on your part may be through ignorance rather than deliberate fraud.

Most external accountants will make it clear that they are not checking for fiddling by staff and therefore this responsibility will still sit with you. However, if they find something you should know, they are very likely to tell you about it.

Wellington Coaching Ltd
Accountants' Report

Accountants' report to the directors of
Wellington Coaching Ltd

You consider that the company is exempt from an audit for the year ended 31st December 2013. You have acknowledged, on the balance sheet, your responsibilities for complying with the requirements of the Companies Act 2006 with respect to accounting records and the preparation of accounts. These responsibilities include preparing accounts that give a true and fair view of the state of affairs of the company at the end of the financial year and of its profit or loss for the financial year.

In accordance with your instructions, we have prepared the accounts which comprise the Profit and Loss Account, the Balance Sheet, the Cash Flow Statement and the related notes from the accounting records of the company and on the basis of information and explanations you have given to us.

We have not carried out an audit or any other review, and consequently we do not express any opinion on these accounts.

Wellington Consulting Ltd
Accountants

PO Box 3425
Wokingham
RG41 2ZY

Directors' Report

This is a report relevant to limited companies only. It is not required for management purposes, only for published accounts.

The key parts are that it states what the company does, how it has done over the last year, what future development plans it has.

The report will also list the directors who have served during the year with dates or appointments and resignations. This information is also available directly from Companies House at no charge (currently).

The amount that the company has spent on research and development and charitable and political donations also has to be declared, unless it is a very small amount.

As with many of these compulsory reports, the exact content will depend on how relevant the information is to the reader of the accounts and the size of the business.

Cash Flow Statement

For smaller companies this is not required but can be a very useful report. It can be produced for non companies where there is no legal requirement.

It answers the question I have often been asked by clients – 'If the company made so much money, why isn't my bank balance bigger?'

As discussed earlier in this book and in more detail in my next one, paper profits can be as a result of raising lots of sales invoices that haven't been paid yet. Alternatively, you may have bought lots of materials but not yet paid your suppliers as you haven't got the 'cash'.

Cash Flow Statement
For the year ended 31st December 2013

	2013 £	2012 £
Cash generated from operations		
Operating profit	67,436	45,422
Reconciliation to cash generated from operations:		
Depreciation	3,000	2,250
Decrease/(increase) in stocks	50	(1,200)
Increase in debtors	(204)	(129)
Increase in creditors	611	105
	70,893	46,448
Cash from other sources		
Interest received	46	36
Dividends received	236	255
New long-term bank borrowings	0	10,000
Proceeds from sale of tangible fixed assets	3,500	0
	3,782	10,291
Application of cash		
Interest paid	(693)	(745)
Tax paid	(13,457)	(9,466)
Dividends paid	(60,000)	(36,000)
Purchase of tangible fixed assets	(8,500)	0
Repayment of amounts borrowed	(2,500)	(2,500)
	(85,150)	(48,711)
Net (decrease)/increase in cash	(10,475)	8,028
Cash at bank and in hand less overdrafts at 1 January	12,444	(2,477)
Cash at bank and in hand less overdrafts at 31 December	1,969	12,444
Consisting of:		
Cash at bank and in hand	1,969	13,544
Overdrafts	0	(1,100)
	1,969	12,444

The cash flow statement, historically also called the source and application of funds, bridges the gap between the profit and the cash.

In simple terms it takes each of the headings in the balance sheet and states whether they have increased or decreased. If you don't owe your suppliers as much, you must have used cash to pay them off. If your customers are taking longer to pay, the cash is currently sitting in their bank account, not yours. Tax paid and loans repaid are common headings which are forgotten when wondering why all the profit is not sitting in the bank.

Every accountant should be able to produce this statement for you. It can make interesting reading and certainly does answer the question – where has the cash gone?

I feel it is so important that I have dedicated a chapter just to this – so keep reading.

Notes to the accounts

Whether the accounts are for your own use, or for publication, it can get very crowded trying to put everything onto a single page.

As referred to above, some items will be demoted to the notes so that more detailed information can be given. This can take the form of a breakdown of the figure or words to support and inform the reader of the context.

If the accounts are for publication at Companies House or the benefit of shareholders and HMRC, there are certain minimum notes that must be included. One note that is important to recognise is the post balance sheet events note. This should make readers aware of anything material that has happened between the accounts date that the accounts were made up to, and the date the accounts were prepared.

If the accounts are not for a company or for HMRC purposes, the choice is yours as to the level of detail shown within the notes, or on the face of the financial statement.

Over time you will start to decide what forms a useful management pack when you review the figures each month. You might think this doesn't sound like you at the moment, but as you start to use this book to help you review what you have in place currently you may start to ask questions, as what has gone before will have an impact on what happens next.

ABBREVIATED ACCOUNTS

This is the term used for the accounts that a limited company has to provide to Companies House each year.

So as not to compromise business by making public commercially sensitive information, you do not need to send in a full set of accounts.

As with most statutory reporting, the exact content will depend on the size of the business and whether it is part of a larger group.

In the case of a small company, you only need to send in the summarised balance sheet, directors' report and selected notes. Anyone looking at the accounts will be able to see the level of assets and debt the company has, but will not be able to see what the turnover was in the year, for example.

If you wish to make public all information in the full accounts, there is nothing to stop you; I would only ask the question, why would you?

SUMMARY

Different trading styles such as sole trader and limited company will have different headings to use and slightly different formats.

When it comes to the accounts for internal use, the main point to consider is what is of benefit to you? As time goes by, there may be some figures where a further breakdown would be useful. With others, the total will tell you what you need to know.

It won't take long for you to decide what your monthly management 'pack' will consist of. If you are finding some reports are of no use, drop them, there is no point taking time producing something that is not used.

The 'pack' of information is for your use, if it doesn't suit, change it until it does. If you bought a motorcycle crash helmet that kept falling over your eyes, would you keep using it? If the accounts are supposed to protect you from the unforeseen, change them until they do.

My one request is schedule in when you are going to look at the accounts, later won't do.

4 Different types of tax

Tax changes on a regular basis, so what follows, by nature of this book, is not year specific but addresses some of the areas I am asked about. Also, for those who don't know what they don't know and, therefore, do not ask, what follows may allow you to ask the right questions and stop you from getting in a mess!

EMPLOYMENT

If you are employed, you fall within the PAYE scheme. This does not mean you automatically pay tax, it means your earnings have to be reported by your employer to HMRC. Historically this was done once a year, but this has now changed. New rules are being introduced so that the employer has to update HMRC once a month.

Depending on what HMRC have on record about your other earnings, be it from other employers, pensions, your own business etc., they will then send a notice of coding to the employer or pension provider to let them know how much tax to deduct each month or week when you get paid.

When a new employee starts work, a form P45 should be given to you. This will have been prepared by the last employer. If one is not available, you need to ask for a P46 to be completed and signed. Using either the tax code on the last P45, if issued in the current tax year, or a P46 where the employee states their current work situation, an initial code number can be found and this will be used until an update is received from HMRC.

Historically the records for an individual were not always linked as they should have been so HMRC were not always working with the full picture. As a result, employees suddenly got large tax bills or repayments from earlier years when the new computer system was installed and records began to be correctly linked and showed errors. The intention is that by having monthly reporting, any errors should be spotted more quickly and large corrections can be avoided.

As an employer, the amount deducted from staff, and needing to be paid as an employer, must be paid over to HMRC. The frequency will depend on the size of the bill and the number of staff the business employs.

Income tax

When calculating how much tax to deduct, the employer should use the tax code provided on the P45 or indicated by the P46. Either of these forms is sent to HMRC when a new employee starts and an amended notice of coding may be issued.

A client recently had a member of staff leave as the employee believed she was paying the wrong tax and thought the employer was to blame. She was paying tax on all her earnings from the employment with my client. Instead of asking, she left. The answer was that she had two part time jobs, but she had not spoken to the tax office and asked for her personal allowance (the amount you can earn before paying tax) to be split across the two employments. My client was correctly calculating the tax as he not been told to do so any differently by the tax office and it was not his business to know how much she was earning in the other job. A simple phone call by the employee to HMRC would have corrected the situation and she would have had a tax refund and not paid tax at either employment as her total earnings were deemed to be below the limit before tax is due. If you have any part-time workers with a second part-time job, you may want to mention this to them.

The opposite situation is where an employee should be paying more tax as they have a company car, for example. This is counted as a non cash benefit, so is the equivalent of an increase in salary, but not in cash. As a result, the tax bill is higher than a purely salary-based calculation. The employer is obliged to notify HMRC; however, the employee can phone HMRC to start the process to make sure the necessary adjustments are done as soon as possible, rather than get a catch-up bill at the end of the tax year.

In summary, the tax code is the key. An employer can only calculate tax based on the code they are given. They cannot apply for a change on behalf of the employee; they can only make sure they fill in their forms correctly.

NIC Class 1

This stands for National Insurance Contributions and is similar to income tax in that it is based on your salary. The contributions that are logged each week/month/year are counted towards your entitlement to pension and other state benefits.

There are different categories which for clarity, or confusion, are referred to by numbers. Employer and employee contribution are known as Class 1.

The big difference between NIC and tax is that tax is cumulative across all employments and sources of income; national insurance contributions are calculated for each employment and for each payment made. If you therefore pay an advance in month one as you were not in a position to properly run the payroll and two months' salary in month two, less the advance, the NIC system will just think that the employee was paid high wages in month two and will calculate the NIC due having no consideration to the fact they were not paid last month. This would cost you and the employee extra money. The correct treatment would be to correctly work out the pay for each month, add the two net figures together and deduct the advance. This is an example of when problems occur when time sheets don't get authorised and someone says they will just deal with it next month. The tax bill would be the same because it is cumulative; the NIC bill would be different.

If any employee earns just enough across two jobs so that when the two incomes are added together they have to pay tax, the chances are that at this low level, there would be no NIC to pay at either employment as they are both under the threshold.

Employer

As things currently stand, an employer must pay a contribution based on percentage of earnings for each employee. No payment will be due for very small weekly amounts, but once the pay for an employee is above approximately £150, the rate is close to 14% of the gross earnings. This calculation is needed for each employee. You will need to check with the HMRC's website to find the exact figure for any particular year.

Even if an employee is over retirement age, the employer must still pay the employee NIC.

Employee

The employee will also have to pay a percentage from gross earnings once they get above the minimum level. The only good thing is that there is a higher level cap after which the rate of contribution reduces.

If the employee has reached retirement age, they can be exempt from this as they are also not entitled to other benefits.

Class 1A

This is a catch-up payment at the end of each year, paid by the employer based on the value of benefits in kind they have paid their staff. At the end of each tax year, a form P11d needs to be completed and sent to HMRC with the payment due. This form will include health insurance, fuel and company car and, potentially, some meals if they have been classed as entertainment/a benefit rather than a necessity.

Benefits

As an employer, there are a variety of state benefits that you may need to pay out to employees to fulfil your legal requirement. I have only listed two of the most common ones below. You may have agreed with your staff to pay above the statutory minimum level of benefit. If you are a small employer, you can claim back many of these costs at a basic level. The definition of small employer can be found on the government website.

Good record keeping of absence and retention of paperwork is essential in this area.

SSP

This is statutory sick pay. If your staff work more than a certain number of hours and get paid more than a certain amount each week and are off work for more than three consecutive days, they may be entitled to this benefit.

If you are paying them anyway, you may be entitled to claim this benefit back to help with their payment.

There is a calculator available on the HMRC.gov.uk website to help calculate this.

SMP

This is statutory maternity pay and HMRC will help pay the costs you have to pay your staff if you are a smaller employer. It may, in some circumstances, be possible to get an advance to help fund the payments.

If you are uncertain how to calculate this, or what the rules are, it is always worth asking advice. You don't want to pay it if you shouldn't and can't claim it back. The reverse is also true; if you should be paying it, you don't want to get caught up in an investigation and penalties when the employee is not at work and has the time to seek advice.

Others

There are a wide range of benefits such as paternity pay for new fathers, adoption pay and others. Some have very strange small print, so allow yourself plenty of time to understand your responsibility. The chances are the employee either won't know and will expect you to, or will have sought advice and try to tell you. As you don't always know where that advice has come from, think before you trust it and do your own research.

Pension

This is nothing to do with tax but remember that if you are looking at the cost of taking staff on, the employer's pension contribution is another factor to consider when calculating the cost of staff.

Self employment and partnership income

This is the responsibility of the individual and is typically paid in three amounts. The first is a half the tax bill based on last year's income due on 31st January. The second payment is the second half based on an estimate of last year's earnings. This payment is due by 31st July. In January of the next year, the third payment is due which will be the correction between the estimate and the actual figures now that they are known. The actual payment amount will typically also include the first half of the following year's tax and so the cycle continues, using the two payment dates of January and July.

When to pay tax due on your income

31st January 2013	Pay any outstanding tax for income for the year to 5th April 2012
	Pay half of the estimated tax bill relating to income for the year to 5th April 2013. The estimate is based on tax paid against the income for the year ended 5th April 2012.
31st July 2013	The second half of the estimate of tax due for income to 5th April 2013
31st January 2014	Pay any outstanding tax for income for the year to 5th April 2013
	Pay half of the estimated tax bill relating to income for the year to 5th April 2014. The estimate is based on tax paid against the income for the year ended 5th April 2013.
31st July 2014	The second half of the estimate of tax due for income to 5th April 2014

Note: If the estimated tax bill is (currently) under £2,000 you may request for it to be collected using your tax code from your employment or pension income if you have any.

If you expect your income will be less than last year, you can request to use a lower figure for the estimate of tax due. This will reduce your first and second estimated payments. All corrections being made in the following January.

Income tax

To calculate tax due on self-employment and partnership income, the total income including rental income, dividend income and bank interest all needs to be added together and allowable deductions made. From the resulting total figure, your personal allowance (the amount you can pay before paying tax) will be deducted as adjusted where permitted e.g. for pension contributions.

The resulting figure will then be matched against the various bands and rates of tax until the total tax bill is arrived at. Any tax that you have already paid, such as an earlier payment or tax deducted from dividends, will then be used to reduce the balance of tax due.

National Insurance Class 2

This was historically known as the stamp, as you went to the Post Office and bought a stamp which was stuck on the card, similar to a savings card. It is a fixed weekly rate so that even if you make a loss, you are contributing something to the welfare and benefits system and your future pension.

The payment is often collected by direct debit either monthly or quarterly, but you can get a bill if they find you should have declared and have not.

If your business is very small, you can elect not to have to make this weekly contribution.

National Insurance Class 4

As with employees' national insurance contributions, this is calculated by a percentage calculation on earnings by way of profits. The first band is calculated at nil, the second at one rate approximately 9%   and the third at a reduced rate. As always, check on the HMRC website for the current rates.

Unlike employment, if you have different self-employed businesses and partnership incomes, the profits from all will be added together for this calculation.

If HMRC get it wrong, they will send you a bill. If you appeal, they sometimes say that you should have understood it, ignorance is not an excuse. If you are not sure seek help; it can work out cheaper than penalties and fines and you can sleep better.

National Insurance Class 3

Just to complete the picture, you can choose to make a voluntary contribution. This is most common where the individual is abroad or taking time out and they can choose to pay a weekly sum to ensure their entitlement to benefits etc. is not compromised.

CORPORATION TAX

This is basically income tax, but for a company. The rate will depend on the amount of profits being taxed.

In a similar way that an individual will have all earned income added together to work out how much tax to pay, so a company will have to add all earnings across the group if there are connected companies.

As discussed in the last chapter under balance sheet/current liabilities/corporation tax, the calculation is not done on the profit in the accounts. The tax office have their own rules about certain calculations, such as how long assets will last, and therefore you may need help in performing this calculation.

To add to the potential complexity of calculation, any rate changes always take effect from 31st March so if your company's year end is a date other than this, the calculation has to be performed by splitting the profit on a daily basis either side of the date and then using the correct rate for each part of the profit. By now, you may be confirming in your own mind why you did not become an accountant!

Please don't let this put you off. You are good at what you do, and there are times when you should get a professional in to help. I certainly do not try to put fillings in my own teeth but I do clean them regularly so that I can reduce the amount of professional help I need and seek help before the situation gets out of control.

The size of your profits and the company will dictate when your corporation tax is due. The good news is they do send a letter and a reminder. This does, however, give you no excuse. For smaller companies it is currently nine months after the year end so you need to put this into your cash flow and make sure you put money aside.

VAT

This is the abbreviation for Value Added Tax in the UK. It is basically a sales tax and will be known by different names in different countries. It is TVA in France, standing for Taxe sur la valeur ajoutée. In Scandinavia it is MOMS, which stands for Mervärdesskatt in Sweden, or Meromsætningsafgift in Danish. Thankfully this book is aimed at the UK so I will focus on this.

Everyone will have to pay VAT on some things they buy as an individual and as a business. However, not everyone has to charge VAT. Whether you have to or not will depend on what you are selling, and how much.

Registration

It is up to the business to register otherwise it can be liable for penalties and paying over the money it did not charge its customers. In some circumstances, the authorities will link businesses to look at the total sales figure so it is important that you monitor it. If you think you are going to exceed the registration limit you have 30 days to let them know. The deceptive thing is that the calculation is based on a rolling twelve months, so waiting until the end of the year when your accountant does your figures is too late. You need to monitor sales every month.

Some businesses with a smaller turnover may choose to register to make themselves appear larger than they are. Alternatively, a franchise may have it as a condition of operation regardless of your turnover.

Much earlier in this book I said you should monitor sales so you know how your business is doing and what cash you have coming in. You also need to do this for the taxman if you are a growing business.

Registration is a simple process but there are sometimes opportunities that you can only take advantage of when first registering, so it is worth seeking advice before doing so.

Rates of VAT

There are a variety of rates of VAT and occasionally these change. In simple terms there is a standard rate which applies to most things, there is a reduced rate which only applies to a few things, and there is a zero rate which applies to essentials such as raw food like oranges. However, orange juice is charged at standard rated VAT as it is processed. Water from the tap is zero, but bottled water is standard rated. It is not always easy to know.

There is also a rate known as exempt which applies to items

which will never be charged VAT. Postage and insurance are examples of this. However, special delivery next day is standard rate as it is a special service. Also, insurance, when recharged to a pub by the brewery, is the service of providing the insurance which is also standard rated. Rent for the pub is standard as it is for commercial premises, the rent for the flat above the pub is exempt as it is a domestic dwelling.

The other two categories that you will come across are outside the scope, including wages, as they are nothing to do with VAT and are not registered where the provider of the service or goods has such a low turnover that they do not have to register and therefore do not have to charge VAT.

The effect of having a turnover below the threshold is that the business does not have to charge VAT (currently 20%). The moment they exceed the threshold their prices all need to go up by this amount if they are to keep the same net sales. If they are supplying individuals rather than VAT registered businesses, the customers cannot claim it back. For some smaller businesses, this is therefore a consideration as to whether they want to expand and then lose business as a result of being more expensive than the smaller trader down the road. I had one colleague who only worked eleven months of the year to make sure she kept below the threshold as most of her clients were small businesses and not VAT registered.

Output tax

This is based on sales you make. It is a percentage depending on what you are selling. As the definition can be difficult in, for example, the construction industry, it is worth asking advice if you are unsure.

If you are supplying goods or services outside the UK, see below.

Input tax

This is the amount you pay when the business pays for goods and services. See above for the rates that you will be paying.

VAT on overseas sales and purchases

If you are VAT registered and buying or selling to businesses abroad, you may be able to not pay or charge the VAT.

If you can give and receive a VAT number and put it on the invoice, you do not have to charge or pay VAT. The idea being that your supplier would have to declare he had sold it to you, and you would then want to claim it back, but as it is cross-border with different rates, it is easier to call it quits and both declare the transaction but neither account for, or claim, VAT.

If you are shipping goods outside the EU, the paperwork increases and needs to be precise as you will need to prove they left the country before getting to the customer. Most international carriers can help in this area. Alternatively, speak with HMRC but leave plenty of time and I suggest you get any decisions in writing which may not be easy.

If you do have to pay VAT on any overseas purchases, you may be able to claim the VAT back from the foreign government but it could take between two months and two years to get the money back. This is not an exaggeration; it is what is quoted on some websites. I have known it take a year from Belgium. Thankfully their government does use email, the challenge is that my German and Flemish are non-existent and my French is poor.

If you purchase large items or goods for resale from outside the EU, you may get a VAT bill when the goods land at port and they cannot be released until the VAT and potential import duty are paid. Make sure this is added to your calculations of price and cash flow.

Accounting for VAT

The simplest form of accounting for VAT is that you pay the difference between the VAT you have invoiced customers and the VAT you have recorded on purchases you have made.

As you are working on paper in and paper out, this is known as the accruals method and it is the most common and compulsory for larger firms.

To help smaller firms, there is also the option to work on a cash basis. You can claim VAT only on bills you have actually paid, but you do not have to hand over the tax you have charged customers until the customers have actually paid you.

If you get a big bill in, you cannot just swap between the two methods. Having decided on the one that suits your business, you need to continue with it unless your growing turnover prevents you from doing so.

Special schemes

There are special schemes such as annual accounting to help even out seasonal trends. For example, monthly accounting if you are always in a repayment situation (typically because you are selling zero rated goods) and flat rate schemes to cut down on the checking HMRC needs to do.

With all special schemes you need to apply for them and be approved, so thought and application are needed.

The flat rate scheme means that although you charge all customers the full amount of VAT, you only have to pay HMRC a flat percentage of gross sales. This percentage will depend on the type of business and is based on a table published by HMRC. You cannot claim VAT on most of your purchases.

Partially exempt

If everything you sell is exempt, that is easy, you can claim nothing.

If some of what you sell is exempt, you cannot claim the input VAT to related purchases.

The calculation is therefore not easy, but once you have a system in place it is easier going forward.

SUMMARY

This book has been written in 2012 so all references are current. The HMRC website (www.hmrc.gov.uk) will allow you to check on current rates and rules.

Although I have mentioned capital allowances, these are to do with taxation rather than understanding your accounts. As the rules change often, I would suggest you seek help in this area.

As an employer, staff will expect you to understand. It is for your benefit as well, so if you need to ask, you could always phone HMRC. They are based in the UK, but their employees have varying levels of experience, so don't be afraid to say you don't understand or ask to speak to their team leader.

Taxes are not complex, it is the accuracy of the information that causes most problems, and the ability to know when to add incomes together, and when not. Once you understand this, you will be fine until they change the rules.

5 Links between the numbers

When presented with a set of accounts, an accountant will instinctively start to do very simple calculations on the numbers. Is the company viable? Can it afford to pay its suppliers and staff? Can they afford to pay the accountant's bill? To be honest the last question is somewhat tongue in cheek. Most accountants are happy with numbers and therefore will do certain simple ratios without even realising they have done them.

As a business owner you need to know what those ratios are. Whether it is an accountant advising you or a supplier or finance house looking to give you credit, understanding what they are looking at and how it looks for your business is key. Even if the numbers look bad, you need to know that is how other people will see them. Having your excuses ready is much better than looking blank and making up irrelevant excuses.

For example, it may look like the business was owed a lot by your customers, but since then, one customer representing a third of the amounts due, has paid. That would sound fine to anyone reviewing the figures. It is simple to say and understand and confirms you have control and know what is going on.

Typically, people reviewing figures know they are looking at historic figures and will accept excuses – or shall we call them reasons. They may ask for an updated set of figures, so make sure any undesirable situations are resolved. I recently had a request for this from an insurance company for one of my clients who had a fire and was making a claim for loss of profits.

What follows are some of the calculations an accountant will do without thinking. It comes naturally to them, in time you will find yourself doing the same. If someone looking at the figures does not make the next three calculations/headings, I would question how seriously they were reviewing your figures. I am not saying they need to take their calculators out, simply thinking that three-something, is bigger than two-something. If you know what others are looking at, you can forewarn them and have the answers ready if what they find is undesirable. More importantly for your own benefit, you will understand what is happening within your business.

CAN YOU AFFORD TO PAY?

This is often the first question anyone looking at the accounts will consider. As a result, you must understand both the result and the calculation that has gone into it.

The reason people ask this is primarily because they want to know if the business will be there tomorrow. Whether they are a customer placing an order, a supplier delivering goods or a prospective employee handing their notice in from their current job and looking to commit to you, they will want to know you will be there next month and beyond.

What follows are the types of tests that bankers will do before extending an overdraft. If you can keep an eye on these and make sure they look 'good', you can present a set of figures that you know will be acceptable and allow you to move to the next stage, whether getting a credit account with your supplier, employing staff who are prepared to do research before the interview, or keeping your bank overdraft.

Liquidity

This is a term commonly used by those in the know. In simple terms it answers the question: has your business got enough funds to pay the bills? Funds are defined as cash, stock and amounts owed by customers and any amounts that you have paid in advance such as insurance. So, if you were to cease trading today and sell off your stock, this would realise cash. Your stock, as valued in the accounts, should be at cost or net realisable value, so the figure you get for it should be at least the figure in the accounts. In practice we know that where there is a forced sale, this would not usually be the case. Accounts are prepared on the assumption that the business will continue; this is known as a going concern basis.

The amounts owed by your customers, and shown in the accounts should exclude any amounts that you know are never going to be paid, i.e. bad debts. Depending on your industry, it may be that you expect a proportion will not pay up. In this case there should be an adjustment known as provision for bad debts. This may be a percentage of sales, or it may be that a couple of customers are doubtful and therefore you can discount these.

Cash is the easiest to define, being cash at bank, in the till and in savings accounts.

The amounts you owe suppliers and others will include any bank overdrafts, credit cards, debts to the taxman such as VAT and PAYE and amounts for which you have not yet received the bill, but have received the service or goods (accruals).

Excluded from this calculation are all the long term things such as vehicles, buildings, mortgages and similar.

So, a company is liquid if it has enough funds to pay all its current debts. This is a figure that the banks will look at when considering overdrafts or loans and suppliers will review when deciding whether to allow you to open a credit account. Also, customers may consider it to ensure that if they pay up front, you will still be there to deliver the goods. In truth, the answer is not just yes, but expressed as a fraction of how many times the business could pay.

Many businesses continue to trade when they are in a negative position as they know it is only a temporary shortfall, others because they are optimistic, others because they have trusting bank managers or the banks have an undertaking from the directors or owners that they will make up any shortfall.

Acid test

This is very similar to the liquidity test except it excludes stock. It takes the view of whether you could collect all the monies owed to you, together with money you have in the bank and pay all debts. It is a very simple calculation but the result is very revealing about how the business is being run.

If you do not yet have your current figures available, just take a look at the last ones sent to the taxman. If you are a very small sole trader business, these figures may not have been submitted but they should be considered for every business.

Overdraft / funding limit

The one thing that the above tests don't show is the overdraft limit. As a business owner, you should know what yours is. An outside observer will not know whether you have exceeded the limit or have considerable head space.

The same is true if some of your funding is coming from elsewhere. You may have an investor who is putting in tranches of cash as they are needed. If this is the case, I would normally recommend a mention of the fact in the accounts so readers have the full picture.

One of the quickest ways to shut a business down is to pull the plug on the overdraft. Banks do not like to do this as the chance of getting their full money back is often very slight. They may, however, discuss the possibility of turning a large overdraft into a loan with fixed repayments. Providing you can find the extra money to make the repayments, it should be considered. At least you won't be paying interest on the overdraft each month. This rate is usually higher than for a loan. If you can't find the money for the repayments, should you still be continuing to trade?

HOW MUCH CREDIT ARE YOUR CUSTOMERS TAKING?

All businesses have credit terms they give to their customers. It may be payment in advance, on receipt, or a number of days after the sale has taken place. It always surprises me when I receive an invoice that does not state on it when the supplier is expecting to be paid.

What you say to customers and what they do may not be the same. It may be they like to pay their bills early, have forgotten and not paid yours, or have not got the funds to pay and are working on the basis of he who shouts loudest gets paid first.

As a business grows, it is easy to focus on sales rather than the collection of money from customers and the longer it is left, the more difficult it can become to collect the debt.

Debtor days

This is another calculation an accountant will tend to do very approximately when first looking at accounts, as the impact of having money sat with customers and not in your bank means you cannot use it to fund future sales.

Like many calculations the maths is simple. Take the amounts customers owe you, divide it into the total sales for the year and multiply the answer by 365.

An example would be if the amount owed by customers was £3,000 and sales for the year were worth £12,000, customers would be taking approximately three months to pay, or 91.25 days. I accept this does not account for growth of sales over the last twelve months, or seasonal trends if you only sell Christmas trees, but this is why understanding the figures is so important. Anyone can apply the formula and get a result, but what it means and what to do about it is what you need to consider.

Percentage of sales

This is similar to debtor days but using the result of amounts owed by customers over total sales as a percentage.

Certain industries will have common percentages and if you are running a retail outlet, it might be zero as all your customers pay for goods at the point of sale, or before.

You need to compare what you are offering customers to

what they are taking. Have your terms changed or are they just stretching what you offer?

Cost to them vs. cost to you

If you cannot afford to buy something, do you place the order? In business, some will. They feel that they need it so they must have it. Payment does not always seem to come into the equation.

If you insist on payment, how much will it cost them to put it on their credit card? If they do not clear the card, they will be paying interest to the credit card company. The important thing is that you have the money owed to you.

If you do take credit cards, remember there are the costs of the terminal rental plus a transaction cost. Although there are deals about, if you only want to take a couple each month, you might consider asking them to pay via PayPal. You will incur a transaction cost but you will get the money and the debt will be cleared. There is a sliding scale so you need to look at the cost per transaction versus the volume to see whether this method of collecting money is cost effective.

The other hidden cost to you is the time you or your staff spend chasing the amount once it is overdue. Although email is cheaper than post, there is still the time and effort that could be better spent towards the next sale, not trying to collect money from the last one.

Can you afford to finance others?

As long as the money is in your customer's account, it is not in yours. You cannot spend the money; you may be paying overdraft interest as the money is not yet in your account. You may find yourself in the position of needing to pay for goods and services using your credit card, all because your customer has not paid.

A simple question to ask yourself is how easy do you make it for them to pay? What are the penalties for not paying on time? I operate a penalty of 10% per month, this builds up pretty fast. You should not be looking at this as an additional source of income as there is no guarantee that it will ever come in. I have had this interest upheld by the small claims court, but then the question follows as to whether the business has the money to pay.

If your customer requests 90 days credit as a condition of placing the order, make sure you can afford to be without the cash for that long. You may suggest a penalty if the debt gets to 91 days and has not been paid, you may also choose to send them a reminder just before the 90 days are up. What you don't want to find is when you chase at 100 days they raise a query which then takes another month to get resolved because it has already been over three months since the sale.

It is possible to do deals for one-off situations but make sure this does not become the norm without you realising it, particularly if your staff know you have done this. They may follow your example without understanding the implications and that you had a good reason on that one occasion.

Potential bad debts

One reason for keeping a careful eye on how much your customers owe you is to prevent bad debts occurring. These can occur when the customer is not able, or not willing, to pay you. If it is simply that they don't want to pay, you need to find out why and see what you can do to change their mind.

If they cannot afford to pay, you also need to persuade them to change their mind. Or you need to decide whether to have the goods back, agree payment terms over a longer period, or take them to court to get the money. If it gets to this stage, consider whether they do actually have the money as you don't want to pay out further money just to have them close the company.

This has happened to me. I was owed nearly £30,000 when I had taken 'on account' amounts for a year, decided that it could not continue and demanded the full amount outstanding. I engaged a solicitor to take the firm to the County Court and about two weeks before the hearing date, I was offered £5,000 to be paid off at £500 per month otherwise they would liquidate the company and I would get nothing. I was left with little choice.

The next time it looked like this might happen was with a different customer who had lost a contract on which they relied. I made sure I chased as soon as the monthly payment was late and made my position clear by withdrawing my services. I did lose some money, but far less and I was free to use my time billing people who would pay.

Remember, if you are honestly not going to get paid, don't leave it in the books and keep fooling yourself and others. Review what has happened and what could be done to ensure it does not happen again.

WHAT PAYMENT TERMS ARE YOU ACTUALLY RECEIVING?

So, we have reviewed the position regarding your customers, but how do you treat your suppliers? Do you pay before the money is due, exactly on the day or when you get round to it?

Obtaining a credit account

One way to make your cash go a little further is to open credit accounts with your main suppliers. This works particularly well if you buy from them on a regular basis. To have the flexibility of ordering when you need to and paying, typically once a month, cuts down on the costs of payments as well as being more convenient. If you are writing cheques out this may be costing you upwards of £1 a time; debit cards cost less but it is still a cost each time you make a transaction rather than one per month.

I sometimes get the response that it doesn't matter because you get free banking. This may be true for now but will not always be the case with the provider.

Some suppliers want you to trade with them for a specific period before they will open a credit account. It may take them a couple of weeks to check you out, so getting the wheels in motion sooner rather than later gives you flexibility. Just because you have a credit account doesn't stop you buying from others if you can get a better price but it does give you the option of delaying payment.

Actual payment terms

Do you know what the actual payment terms of your suppliers are? If you don't know, how do you know if you are paying on time?

Some suppliers may want the sale enough to give you extended terms but you won't know unless you ask. I recently wanted to take up an offer but knew I would not be in a position to use the service for three months. I therefore asked if I could pay a deposit and not pay the balance for three months. Much to my surprise they agreed without question. If I hadn't asked, I would not have got 90 day terms.

I notice a wide range of attitudes to paying bills amongst my clients. Some are good and pay on receipt of the invoice, some pay within a week of it being due. I have one who pays a monthly sum off her old account and some who pay monthly towards the next lot of work. I also have a couple who are good at promises and apologies and will be getting invoices for late payment interest soon.

Creditor days

This is the amount you owe suppliers over the amount you have purchased in the year multiplied by 365. An example would be that you buy £120,000 worth of goods in the year and at the end of the year, you owe suppliers £20,000. This would mean you owed for two months' (60 days) worth of purchases. A straightforward calculation, but its accuracy will depend on whether you are including two similar figures. The amounts you owe suppliers may include advertising and other service-related purchases, whereas the figure taken for purchases is often seen as the cost of goods sold. To be accurate, you would need to exclude expenses when comparing with purchases or include the expenses in purchases. As with the aged debt report for customers, reviewing the report in detail will be more beneficial than just looking at total figures.

To be accurate in this calculation you may need to carefully define what is and isn't to be included. The outside reader of the accounts will not have this luxury and therefore will be taking the figures at face value and making judgements on this basis.

Anyone looking to give you a credit account may ask for sight of your accounts as they will want to see how you are treating other suppliers before they technically lend you money by letting you have the goods before paying for them.

Flexibility

As I mentioned above, if you don't ask, then you won't get. Most suppliers would rather engage in a dialogue and know that you wanted time to pay, or you wanted to make a part payment with the rest to follow later rather than be fobbed off or left in the dark.

Interest

Who would you rather pay interest to, your suppliers or your bank? Consider what rate each may be charging and remember the cheapest option may be to make sure your customers pay you on time, then you will have the cash to pay your suppliers.

Discount

You may find you are being offered a settlement discount. This may be another way to reduce bills and contribute towards the cost of funding the cash you use to pay them.

I have had some clients who placed an order and never looked at the invoice for a month, whereas if they had diarised to pay in fourteen days, they could have saved 10%. If that had been offered to them at the point of order, they would not have ignored it.

RETURN ON INVESTMENT (ROI)

This term is often used in larger businesses or by sales people trying to justify the cost. That is fine, it is the right thing to do if all the costs are being considered, but for those looking at a high level, certain costs do get forgotten. A typical example will be the time lost to productive work by staff attending training required on a new system or piece of equipment.

If you know how to calculate ROI you can satisfy yourself that your decision will be based on making a positive return from the money you are spending.

What is it?

When you spend money, you expect to get something for it. When you invest money you expect to get back more money than you put in. With a savings account it is straight forward as you will be told the interest rate when you open the account, and as it changes. In business it is not so straight forward.

If you employ a telesales company to make calls for one week, how many sales will they need to make to cover the cost of employing them? Remember it will not be the value of the sales; it is the profit on each sale that needs to be recognised to justify the expenditure. Here we are talking about actual invoiced sales, not just warm prospects.

How do you calculate it?

Look at the costs involved. In the case of my telesales example, it is not just the cost of hiring the firm, are they going to be using your phones or theirs? Who is going to obtain the names and numbers of people they will be calling? Are you going to need to buy in lists? What sort of briefing are they going to need? Are you going to be spending a week writing scripts for them and building up their product knowledge?

The other part of the calculation is how much extra profit you will make as a result of this activity. As overheads such as rent would be incurred regardless, you could justify leaving that out of the calculation if you are preparing the calculation for an activity rather than the whole business. Costs such as the items being sold, their shipment, transaction charges for accepting payment, must be included as these are all generated by the extra sales.

Having decided on the costs and the contributions from additional sales, you can then work out how much more you will get than you paid out. This is the return on investment.

What activity can you think of where you can identify the costs of that activity and the extra profits as a result of that activity? The challenge is breaking the costs and income down so they can be linked to that discrete outlay.

Over what time frame?

Following on from my telesales example, you need to be clear about the time frame for your calculation. It may be that the contribution from sales made during the one week do not cover the costs related to hiring the telesales team but, as customers have signed up to a monthly purchase, or history says that 50% of customers will buy again once they have sampled the product, the costs may be worth covering to get the return over the longer term.

Another example may be a plumber who decides to get his qualification for working with gas. The qualification may cost several thousand pounds and he will lose a week of work while he is attending the course. The question is how much extra work, or higher priced work, will he be able to get as a result of having the qualification?

Although these are small examples, the same applies to a national firm investing in an additional site. What are the costs of the site? These need to include renting or buying, fitting out, stocking, staffing, running costs, marketing the new location, updating existing marketing material including web sites... and so the list goes on. Against this, they will need to consider how much more in additional sales they will make and what contribution that would make to profits. How quickly do they expect to recover their costs and actually be making a profit?

Why does it matter?

Every business has limited funds and the question is how best to spend them. Working out what you will get back by committing a sum of money will help you decide what to commit to. This is particularly true when there is a choice about what to spend the money on, or if you are getting finance, how much to get.

When speaking to marketing people, one of their biggest frustrations is that businesses buy advertising but then don't track the response from each source. When you purchase something, how often are you asked where you saw the advert or why you chose that supplier? It is becoming more common with computers as you can automate the question or build in other methods to track where the sale came from. Without the aid of a computer, how do you know what advertising is working and which is not? Is the part that is apparently not working actually raising your profile and prospects' awareness, and is the marketing that invites them to buy actually only tipping the balance? Returns from marketing can be one of the most difficult figures to accurately measure.

Some returns cannot always be measured in cash but if they can be, they should be. Upgrading your customer services should result in happier customers. Happy customers could be measured in numbers retained or new customers obtained through referral. These can then be equated to money.

IS IT BETTER TO RENT OR BUY (OR LEASE)?

This is a question I am often asked and the answer, like the answer to many others in this book, is it depends. I have included it here because it is a typical example of why you need to link numbers.

What follows are some of the factors to consider before making the decision. Once you have worked through these it should help with the decision.

Define what you want

The first question is defining exactly what it is that you need and want. The two may not be the same. List why you are looking to make the purchase and what you expect from it. This can be done whether it is new premises, new computer system, or a replacement vehicle.

The next question is how long will it be of use to the business? Computers can become out of date quite quickly but still be serviceable for many years. A business may outgrow its premises, need new space and no longer require the old building. Cars and vans serve a function and it depends on the mileage you intend doing as to how long they might last.

Another linked cost to be considered is the maintenance to keep the purchase in a serviceable condition. Even laser printers can be leased rather than purchased, with servicing and replacement toner, drums etc., all being part of a monthly fee. The lease company would want to know approximately how many sheets you would expect to print per month and, if it is a car, how many miles you would expect to do. With serviced offices the question would be how many staff and what additional services do you want?

Residual value or replacement cost

The factor to consider when purchasing an item is the residual value; what value it will have to the business at the end of its intended life and remembering it will then need to be replaced. To sell a four year-old car and use the funds towards a new one will realise a much higher percentage of purchase price than if you did the same to a four year-old computer. Some lease agreements have clauses built in to say the item will be replaced with a newer model every two or three years. This may or may not be of benefit.

If purchased items break down beyond repair they may be insured, otherwise you may need to find the money to replace them.

Typically, if you are leasing equipment it is never yours and therefore you are basically renting it. You will have nothing to show for it at the end, unless it is a lease purchase arrangement where you make a final large payment to buy it from the lease company. Read the small print.

Methods of funding

As with any personal purchase, the choices are loans from banks or other sources, hire purchase or credit agreements, or simply paying cash.

The big difference between a loan and hire purchase is that you do not own an asset bought on hire purchase until the final payment is made. For the purposes of insurance and care of the asset, it is your responsibility, but if you do not make your payments, the asset can be reclaimed and you will have nothing to show for your payments. In the same way, you cannot sell the asset until the hire purchase agreement is cleared.

Taking on a loan or paying cash means the asset is yours to

do with as you will. You can sell the asset but any outstanding amount on the loan will still need to be paid.

Paying cash prevents you incurring the cost of interest, but means that the cash is not available for other uses.

The method of acquisition can make a big difference to the profit. If, for example, you buy a property, only the interest can be included to reduce the profits, whereas all the rent paid can be offset to reduce your tax. So, it would appear to others that you make more profit if you buy. The truth of the matter is that you might owe money in the short term, but the property is fully under your control and you will have it forever to sell when you want.

In the case of vehicles and other items that wear out (known as depreciation in accountants' speak) there is less of a difference since the amount they reduce in value can be offset against the profits, as well as the interest on the loan. The interest is the one cost you can avoid if you can afford to.

Typically, leasing involves a fixed monthly fee which includes certain running costs and is therefore useful for planning and managing cash flow.

Opportunity cost

This is the cost of not purchasing or renting the item. I have mentioned earlier my client who keeps a pot of cash and can therefore buy engineering equipment from company closures and other cut-price sources. If he was not able to do this, he might be spending more than twice as much again to purchase the kit new.

As an example, if he buys some equipment for £40,000 in an auction that would usually have cost £60,000 at full price, he has saved £20,000 because he had the money ready. So, if he had not had the money because it was sitting in a high interest account, it would have cost him an extra £20,000, less the interest he was earning on that money. This might seem an extreme example, but it demonstrates the principle.

He is only able to go for such good deals because he has the cash ready rather than saying yes, then worrying about cashing in investments or getting a loan to fund them.

The reason it is known as a cost is that it has reduced the profits you could have made. It will not affect the figures on paper and only needs to be considered when looking back at what you could have done if…

When making large purchases, make sure you don't compromise to the extent that securing the next level up could have enabled you to do a lot more. Planning and knowing your intentions is a critical part of the profit making process, so read the next chapter before making the next large purchase.

Available options

Don't assume that you will get funding just because you are in business.

Many small businesses have a poor credit rating. This is not because they are bad payers but because they have no, or very little, credit history.

I have discussed the usual options and there may be more that are available to you such as loans from members of your family. The one point I would make is do not presume where the money will come from.

A client of mine recently wanted to lease a new van. I put him in contact with someone I know who has sourced vehicles for clients before. He was embarrassed to find that the companies he usually used turned down the applications, even for loans, due to his credit history, or lack of. He did buy his van on HP by going direct to Ford and they had no problem as they were treating it as a purchase for an individual, not a business, although they knew it was for business use and my client is a sole trader. The only point I would make is that he is borrowing £14,000 on HP and will be paying back nearly £5,000 in interest over the next four years. For him it is better than not having a van – he is a plumber.

Also, buying the van from new means he is less likely to have large repair bills which he could have done if he had bought a second or third hand one for less. This highlights the need to look at the big picture.

KEY PERFORMANCE INDICATORS (KPI)

Throughout much of this book I refer to the need to monitor: KPIs are commonly used by an organisation to evaluate its success or the success of a particular activity in which it is engaged. They do not have to be financially based, so it could be something like the average length of time your customers have to wait to have their telephone calls answered or returned.

Which should you calculate?

You should calculate anything that you can measure that you can control and might be of use to the organisation.

You may feel that you cannot control many things, such as the weather. You won't be measuring the weather but you can measure the number of lost days of work or extra umbrellas sold. To control these factors, you could have inside jobs as well as outdoor work and move the umbrellas closer to the customer entrance or window when it is raining.

The important factor is that anything you choose to measure is of use to you in moving the business forward. You will find that as your business develops over time, what you want to measure will also change.

Why are they worth calculating?

Once you start gathering the figures you then have a chance to review them. You will see which results are the same as you expected and which are different. I had a perception of how long I spent on the telephone to HMRC. I also have a phone that tells me the call duration. By being able to measure how long I spent on hold, I could easily justify a hands-free phone so that I don't have so much lost time. I can continue with other work while I wait for my call to be answered. Because I can see the information, I now know when it is the best time of day to call HMRC – it does depend on the department!

Another example which may be of interest to my clients is how long after they email me do I reply, or how long after they bring their books in do I offer them their draft accounts for discussion? This is what business is about. Knowing the figures and acting on them.

Have a think about this and decide what would be of interest to you and what you would like to measure that could then help improve your business. Is it sales enquiries converted to paying customers? Is it customer retention? Is it cost of delivery of your product or services? The important thing is what is important to you and your business.

Having decided what information you want, the next step will be to decide how to gather it. Nothing is impossible; it may just be that you need help in putting systems in place to gather the information. I certainly don't know how I would find out how many times my phone rings before it is picked up, but I know who I would ask to help me find out. The same is also true of web enquiries. I could ask customers when they make the enquiry or I could ask my IT guys to tell me what word had been searched for, causing the prospect to click on my site.

First decide what information you want which would be of benefit to improving your business. Then worry about how to capture it.

RETURN ON CAPITAL EMPLOYED (ROCE)

Some business owners invest a lot of their money in their business. For some this can be without realising it. They pay things on behalf of the firm, they buy things because the firm needs them or they put a sum into the business at the start without having drawn up a plan as to the total amount needed.

When you started your business, you should have had some sort of plan: how much you were going to put in and how much you wanted/needed to take out. How close were you to your original plans?

If you had bought premium bonds with the money you have invested in your business, would you be making a better return? There are no guarantees in business or with premium bonds, but you have much more control over your returns from being in business – providing you work at it.

Too many times I have seen someone who has been made redundant fall into business because they cannot get employment as fast as they would like. They fancy the flexibility of self-employment, they buy into a franchise believing that all the difficult bits have been done for them so they can take the short cut to success. With some franchises this may be true, but for many it is purely the structure and possibly the name you are purchasing, you still need to do the marketing, product or service delivery, book-keeping and making sure someone answers the phone.

Whether you have been in business a short or long while, make sure you remember you are running a business to make money at a better rate than keeping the money in a savings account.

Whether you could earn more as an individual being employed by someone else is a different question and is partly about lifestyle and personal choice.

SUMMARY

Building up an understanding of the common ratios means that you will be able to apply them to your business, as well as others.

In most cases, the calculations do not need to be to multiple decimal places, you are just looking to see if the answer is smaller or larger than last time, or simply positive or negative.

When starting to look at the future, recognising all the costs and possible returns enables you to make informed decisions based on facts. My next book looks at planning for the future in much more detail.

To register your interest, leave a message about what would help you at:

www.understanding-accounts.co.uk/book2

6 Where the cash comes from – and goes to

Soon after I started in accountancy, a new standard report was introduced for limited companies know as the Source and Application of Funds Statement. This has since been replaced by the Cash Flow Statement. It shows a record of a company's cash inflows and cash outflows over a specific period of time, typically a year.

Before this formal statement, a few firms were producing something similar for their clients so they could answer this question.

So much for the formal side, most small companies do not have such a statement prepared as it is not required by law, however it is the easiest way to answer the question 'If I have made that much profit, why isn't it sitting in the bank waiting for me to take out?'

By the end of this chapter, you should have a better understanding of the movement of your cash and impact on your business.

WHY CONSIDERING CASH IS IMPORTANT

A saying you may have heard is Cash is King. The reason it is true is that without cash, a business will cease to function. Not necessarily straightaway, but at some point your borrowing will need to be repaid. Whether it is a bank loan or a long term investor, or simply your supplier who has given you 30 days credit, they will want their money.

If you do not even consider the cash implications you may take orders and not be able to buy the goods or pay the staff to fulfil them. Even worse, you may start but not be able to complete a customer's order so the customer won't pay as their purchase is incomplete and your supplier won't supply as they have not been paid. This is the sort of downward spiral that some business owners find themselves in.

From this you can understand why there are certain attractions in being paid up front, before the supply to the customer has started. Again, one can still fall foul by using the cash on running costs and having none left to fulfil the order. That is why it is important to have a plan and check against the plan for both cash and sales.

Without cash a business cannot function

Although bartering may appear to be one way around the

need for cash, not everyone accepts it. In fact, in business, very few do.

A wise coach once asked me, 'Why do you do any work for free? Doesn't your client realise the supermarket charges you cash for your bread so why shouldn't they pay you for what you sell?' Good point; having said that, I still do a few things for free or below full price, but I know that I will be repaid indirectly in the longer term, whether it is word-of-mouth marketing bringing me new clients without heavy advertising costs, or building my reputation, meaning that potential clients will try and find me. Having said this, I still need to pay for my bread so I am careful how much I do without charging full price!

Another point to note is that bartering is not a way to avoid tax. A cash equivalent can be invented by HMRC, so if you don't use the cash figure, they will for their calculations. Bear in mind the figure they invent may be considerably more than you had worked on, but it may not be easy to prove your figure.

So, your suppliers will expect to be paid in cash, or cash equivalents, as will the bank with any loan repayments. Although a business can survive on credit or borrowing for some while, the day will come when these amounts will need repaying.

Coming back to the less extreme viewpoint, money needs to come in to enable money to go out. Yes, that is stating the obvious, but when you start to get involved with the operational detail, the big picture is sometimes lost. When a supplier presses you for payment, don't just send a cheque that will bounce as this might cost you an extra £35 in bank charges. The worst I have seen amongst my clients is a £75 charge per bounced direct debit. This soon adds up and really does compound the situation. As we all know, it is the banks that will help themselves first to their charges ahead of any other amounts you owe.

A word of warning, when I am talking about cash, I mean cleared funds in a bank or cash in the till, not promises of payment such as 'the cheque is in the post'.

If you plan, you can ensure you have sufficient funds

It comes back to the saying that planning prevents poor performance. You may know an extended version of this saying, but I am too polite to include it in print...

What is sufficient?

Until you have created your plan you will not know what sufficient is – exactly. In general terms it will include being able to pay your bills when they are due. The unknown factor will be money in, and as a consequence, that will affect money out. That is why you need a plan.

What sort of plan?

Most businesses should have two types of money related plan, a budget and a cash flow forecast.

The big difference between the two is that the cash flow will have the dates that payments are intended to be made. A budget will be spreading the cost across the period from which you get the benefit. The simplest example is insurance. The cash flow will show the annual premium being paid on one date, the budget will show one twelfth each month.

The order of planning should be that the first draft of the budget is prepared before the cash flow. Unless you know what you need during the year or period, you will not know when it will need to be paid for. Another extreme example is an exhibition, where the desire to go is the first decision, the availability of staff to attend on that date is next, the price is the next piece of information and the payment terms often come last. There may be a 50% deposit due six to twelve months before the event, with the balance due three months before. The benefit will not be felt until the pre-exhibition marketing starts.

The purpose of this book is to help you understand the figures and their relationship. My next book helps you create the plans for both budgets and cash flows.

Who should do the planning?

Most of the staff involved in an organisation could contribute to a plan. The big question is how do you best collect their contributions?

The first stage is to ensure that there is a high level plan. Once this strategic plan is agreed, this can then be shared with the next level.

I often see managers given a budget to work to and then reprimanded when they do not meet it. How much did they contribute to its creation? How much control do they have over the costs within it? To what level have they been educated in basic finance?

Even if your managers are not very experienced, they may well have a worthwhile contribution to make. At the end of the day, it comes down to education and learning what costs are involved and what profits can be made. You have chosen to read this book. You could buy them a copy or send them on a course. Once again, I can recommend a good trainer...

How should you plan?

For many people I speak to, they will know when certain payments such as their car tax are due. They will put money aside towards expenditure on large items such as holidays or will use a budget scheme to spread the cost of necessities such as car insurance or domestic utilities. They know these things have to be paid, so put a plan in place to make sure they are.

Why don't many businesses do the same by making a plan and comparing their progress against it? If I asked you to produce a list of payments that need to be made next January would you know where to find that list? What factors might mean you could not cover all the bills due? Are any of these due in December but you are already deciding will be paid late? What are the penalties? What contingencies do you have in place ready for the unexpected?

If you are the only person in your business, you may be able to use private funds to tide you over for a month if the business is unable to pay you, but do you have sufficient to inject funds in to the business to pay five or 50 staff as your business grows? I feel tempted to say you can get away with it when it is just you, but even that comes to an end at some point.

Another reason to have a plan is to ensure you are making a good decision about how to spend your money. If a 'good deal' comes up, do you have available funds to take advantage of it? If you think you do have enough cash, are you going to actually jeopardise something else you have forgotten you had agreed to do? A plan would have shown you what else was coming up.

Further on in the chapter I will explain about cash flow forecasts, but for now I will just say how having a plan means you will always have the cash. This is because if you are aware you will not have spare cash, you will not overspend.

Cash is how HMRC expect to be paid

Earlier I referred to bartering but one organisation that will definitely not accept this form of payment is HMRC. They want cash, cheque or bank transfer by the prescribed day. In some areas such as VAT, you now have to pay electronically. Gone are the days of running out of cheques and saying you will send it off when the new cheque book arrives. Even losing your card and waiting for a replacement is not an acceptable excuse, it seems. Their assumption is that you can always go to your bank and request they do an electronic transfer – or get someone else to pay providing HMRC get their money.

One good thing about payments to HMRC is that you know when they are due. If you pay all your bills on time there are no sudden surprises. In all honesty, they are one supplier that you really can plan for and rely on to charge you for paying late. The only exception to this is if you leave it until the last minute to prepare your accounts, you won't know how much to plan for.

Fines and penalties

The types of bill you can get from HMRC which can muck up your plans are penalties, fines, surcharges and interest. The one thing all these have in common is that they can be avoided. They can also be planned for. If you are receiving these, there is either a very good reason such as your ex-partner is refusing to sign the accounts or you have not been planning generally and therefore you have received a brown envelope through the door telling you that more money is due now.

If you are happy to pay fines and penalties, could I suggest that you get on top of the task, meet the deadlines, avoid the fines and send me the money you would otherwise have sent to HMRC! Alternatively, you could donate it to charity as that is allowable as an expense to reduce your tax bill whereas fines are not.

As a business you are a tax collector for HMRC

When some people start in business they do not realise they also become tax collectors. I have given an overview of some of the different sorts of tax in this book. For now I shall use Value Added Tax (VAT) for my example.

Once you are registered for VAT, all monies you collect from what you sell or provide include an element that needs to be passed on to HMRC in the form of VAT. I appreciate that there are a few exceptions but the chances are you will already know if these apply to you.

So, when you receive money from your customers how much do you put away ready to hand over to the taxman? Many banks, when opening a business bank account, automatically set up a savings account as well. Few bank managers explain what it is for. They assume you know as you are in, or going into, business. In truth, it might help your cash flow if they made sure you understood the benefit of putting money aside for the taxman. I accept that they are not there to educate their customers but an indication of the benefit of putting money to one side would save their customers sleepless nights in future.

HMRC do understand about cash flow and the one example that makes me smile is that most pubs are given November as the end of their VAT quarter, whenever they register. This means they have to pay their VAT to HMRC at the end of December when they have all their Christmas takings to afford to pay the bill. The next payment to include the high December takings is not due till the end of March, by which time they should have recovered from the usual slow trading in January and February. You could say that it just happens like that – or that the preferred quarter end for that industry was carefully planned to make it easier for the traders to pay their VAT bills. Pubs are traditionally poor at planning their cash flow as they will just claim that trade is unpredictable. What they really mean is that it is cyclical, although I appreciate there are other factors as in all industries.

The other benefit to HMRC is that they can more accurately compare businesses in a similar trade. By each business within a sector having the same quarter end, any factors such as weather or school holidays should affect everyone in that sector to a greater or lesser degree.

Remember VAT is only one tax you need to save for. If you have been employed you may have been taxed under pay as you earn, better known as PAYE. Each time you got paid, you paid some tax. Well actually your employer collected it from all employees and then paid it to HMRC. If you have anyone on the payroll, this applies to you.

Then there is the tax on profits to consider. This is a payment type commonly forgotten when business owners are reviewing their cash needs for the future.

Your track record for cash

Building up a good track record can be key to the business. At the start of this book, I referred to building up a track record as this would form part of your reputation. I also discussed trends and what can impact on the business such as seasonal sales trends and government policy, to name but two. What follows is closely linked to this but looking at purely the cash aspect.

Borrowing ability

Whether you are a sole trader or a limited company, you have a credit file and as such you have a history. Past performance is heavily relied on if lenders are even to consider your application.

Future investor's view

If you are always paying suppliers late, you may find that they require cash with your order in future. With one of my clients she has a rule that if she involves me in chasing an outstanding amount, the customer cannot advertise in her publication again.

For her it is not worth the hassle and the cost of employing me when she has others waiting to take their place. For the late payer, they lose the advertising space to a competitor – as well as getting charged interest for late payment which she rarely waives.

This example may only be on a small scale but if you are looking to set up a supplier account they may well ask for references from your existing suppliers. Are you going to be in a position where you can give them details of your largest suppliers whose feedback will be that you always pay by the due date?

If you have a history of paying on time and make one payment late, you are usually forgiven but it will be noted and can be held against you in future, especially if the company use a credit reference agency such as Experian.

Getting credit for hire purchase and leasing can also be a problem if you are known as a regularly late payer. By planning and creating a perfect track record you may find opportunities are open to you when closed to others. I recently took out a bank loan to develop part of the business. Within two weeks I had a letter to say my company charge card limit had also been increased, without me asking for further credit.

WHERE DOES THE CASH COME FROM?

For some, more cash seems to flow out than in but they still survive. For others, they think they are doing fine but all of a sudden they realise that they can't pay their bills and the banks say 'no more'. Understanding the sources of funds is important as then you know how reliable each source may be with regard to its size and the date to be received. You also know what costs are associated with each source, so you make a business decision rather than grabbing the first option offered.

Sales

Although this is the obvious source of funds for a business, it is not the only one. It should be split further depending on what you are selling and to whom.

Sales of goods and services

By this I mean sales from goods or services that are the primary reason the business is in existence. This should be the main ongoing source of cash and, with the exception of guarantees, should be repeated in the knowledge that the funds do not have to be repaid.

When the cash comes in is a different issue and a critical one. This will be dealt with in the relevant areas.

Within this heading I am covering sales to businesses and consumers, wholesale and retail. This is really what everybody thinks of as sales.

I also refer to my earlier comment that doing some work or donating some goods for free is fine in very small quantities if you are viewing it as a substitute for paying out on advertising. However, as sales of goods and services are the main source of income for most businesses, it is the one source you need to focus on maximising.

Sales of fixed assets

Fixed assets were described in the Reviewing Your Accounts chapter but basically they are the things bought for use within the business which are expected to have a useful life of more than a year.

So, when old office furniture is sold, money comes in to the business. This is a simple example. If the assets sold are of more value than their cost less use to date, i.e. value in the books, then this helps profit. Whether they bring in more or less it is still an inflow of cash: being a cautious accountant I would add the rider, subject to any finance still outstanding that needs to be repaid.

If you are in need of cash, consider whether you are still using all your equipment or whether there is some that can be sold off without compromising the ability of the firm to generate and fulfil future sales. Not only will this generate cash, it will reduce clutter.

When some firms are purchased by others, the main reason is 'asset stripping'. This is where the purchaser knows they can make good money just selling off the capital items (fixed assets) and not bothering to continue with the trade. Or it may be that the purchaser is in the same industry and can absorb all the customers and does not have the need for duplicate equipment. If the business premises includes a property in a desirable area, relocation and then sale of the original property can also realise funds in this situation.

Gifts and donations

Some organisations do not rely on sales, but instead on gifts and donations. Although you might think that the income is less easy to predict, typically certain events will generate certain levels of income. Even where there are factors beyond your control such as the weather, it is possible to insure against having to cancel the event. If you only have one event per year, the cost of the premium may well be worth the 'guarantee' of some income. An example was the Windsor Park sponsored horse ride that had to be cancelled in May 2012 as the ground was too wet. The Lions charity expects a large amount of sponsorship money from this annual event. Insurance was well worth taking out as there was the cost of administration of the refunds to cover with no income.

If your organisation has its total income based on this source, then planning with contingencies is an important factor in guaranteeing the success and continuation of the organisation.

Grants

The availability of these may vary from one year to the next. They can never be guaranteed unless you have full approval in writing with payment dates.

I had one client who was allocated a grant. They had to pay and then claim back the money. They sent in the receipt but as it was late, the grant was not given, although the payment had already been made by them. I would always encourage you to read the small print and diarise all key dates to ensure that this source of cash actually happens rather than just being part of your plans.

Deposits

By this I mean where a customer gives you money up front, i.e. before the service or goods are provided. The one reservation I would make about this is that they may want the cash returned. Whether they can have it back will be down to your terms and conditions. There may be a certain expectation for your industry but that does not mean it automatically applies to you. To safeguard yourself make sure that your customer clearly understands what your policy is, otherwise the cost of court cases to defend a claim can be out of proportion to the deposit taken.

The other thing to remember about deposits is that they are payment for, or towards, a sale so when planning cash, remember not to double count. By this I mean that if you have already taken full payment up front, you cannot expect payment again when the goods or services have been supplied. If you are looking at your sales orders to see how healthy the next few months are, remember to reduce it by the deposits already received when considering the potential cash flow over the coming months.

Interest received

In the current climate, this is not usually a very large figure. For many businesses this might be only a dream as they are more used to paying, rather than receiving, interest.

That fact is it is another source of income. It may be that your business is lending another business funds on which they are paying you interest rather than taking a loan from a bank. The rates you receive can be considerably more than simply keeping the money on deposit. However, you also need to consider the risk and the repayment of the main sum before embarking on this type of lending.

My advice would be to consider it, but tread cautiously and get everything in writing and signed with clauses to cover the worst case scenario. Also, get professional help in setting up the agreement. You would also need minutes of the board meeting approved by the directors, where the loan and its repayment terms are discussed, if you are a limited company. This might seem over the top, but we are looking here at cash flowing in and I would not want you to be caught out by the original lump sum never being repaid.

Within this I would also include any dividend income received from shares held by your business. This may arise due to investments in other related businesses or purely on the open stock market.

If you are getting into this area of investments, I would suggest you seek advice as this is outside the scope of this book.

Rental and other non-trade income

The most common source of non-trading income is letting or sub-letting and receiving rent as a result. This may arise from anything such as spare desks in a serviced office, parking spaces that are part of your property but not required, through to renting out your old premises following your relocation or actually purchasing one or more properties to find tenants for.

If the business owns, or has the tenancy of the property, any rental income will then be counted as part of the total income of the business. If you buy or rent a shop with a flat above, the rent received from the flat would be part of the income of the business even if it was the business owner living in the flat. The rules are slightly different between sole traders and limited companies so check on your particular situation. I do not want to get into how the rent should be calculated, just to say if you don't include it the taxman will and potentially penalise you for not doing so.

Investors

This can be a very good source of cash with the rider that the investor will expect something in return. By its nature, an investment is classed as long term and many people investing in a business will be looking at an on-going income by way of distribution of a share of the profits rather than necessarily a return of the lump sum.

If you are planning on growing your business to the level where it can be sold or traded on the stock market, the investor will be looking at 'capital appreciation'. This means simply an increase in the value of the business as a whole. In the same way some people buy property in the hope that it will increase in value, so investors buy a chunk of your business in the hope that its value will grow.

The cash that an investor puts in can make a huge difference as to how fast you can grow. Typically they will expect to see your plan which I will cover in detail in my next book. What they will be interested to see is how long they have to wait. The important thing here is that you understand the principle.

Borrowing – official

This can be a structured loan plus interest payments with repayments dates. Under this title we are looking at cash coming in. This cash is usually obtained for something specific such as the purchase of equipment, so although it is cash in, the cash out is also part of the plan.

The exception to this is a bank overdraft where it is the facility to work on 'borrowed cash' that allows the business to trade. Overdraft interest is usually more expensive than loan interest so should not be used for specific expenditure unless it is known that it is required only in the very short term.

Two other methods of cash to mention are invoice factoring and invoice finance. Different people use these terms differently. In essence, a factoring company buys your sales invoices from you at less than face value so you get a chunk of money when the invoice is raised. The customer then pays the factoring company, who then pay you the balance less their charges.

It depends on which method you are using as to whether you or the factoring company have to chase the money. As long as it remains unpaid you are clocking up charges with the factoring company. This can be an expensive way of having your cash coming in, but is justified in some cases.

Borrowing – unofficial (late payment)

You may find that you have more available money than you thought but it may be because you have not paid your suppliers. It is therefore not a direct source of cash but has the same effect.

By not paying Company A, you can afford to buy from Company B. Remember that Company A will need paying at some point.

When looking at a year-on-year comparison of figures, the fact that you owe suppliers at the end of this year, more than you did at the end of last year means in theory that you had more cash to use elsewhere. This does not mean you have more overall – just that from a cash perspective, there is more available. To bring this back to a domestic situation, if you have money in your household account, it may be because you have not yet paid the electricity bill that has arrived but is sitting there waiting to be paid. Overall you don't have more, but your bank account still looks like it has a better balance than it will soon, when the bill is settled.

The one thing to watch about this type of cash in, is how much is it costing you? If your suppliers offer an early settlement discount you will be missing out on this, if they charge interest on late paid bills, you will be losing out by having to pay this charge. I charge 10% per month on late paid bills. This might seem high in that if you pay ten months late you will pay more than the same amount again of the original bill. This is high, but I am not a lending institution and when you signed up to work with me, you agreed to the terms on my invoices which were definitely not payment ten months after the invoice date.

If you are going to use this source of cash, just consider how much it is actually costing you.

WHERE DOES THE CASH GO TO?

Many business owners believe they know what they spend their money on. For those who do not track expenditure monthly, it can be a shock at the end of the year when their accountant tells them everything they had forgotten. Alternatively, they don't get as far as the end of the year before they realise they have run out of cash.

I have listed below some major headings, some of which you will think 'of course', and others which you may not have realised eat up your available cash.

Goods for resale

This is probably the most obvious cash out. If you are supplying goods you need to pay for them (I won't say first, as you might be buying for a specific order where the customer has paid cash with the order before you buy in the goods).

Although the level of purchases may depend on the level of sales, one thing is for sure, you should not sell what you cannot provide. Unless you are breeding livestock you will typically have to buy what you will be selling. I appreciate you may be altering it in some way, for example if you buy raw materials, or are writing or publishing a book, the fact remains you will need to buy something if you are selling something.

If you are thinking that you only supply services, I would like to remind you that you and your staff would like paying for their time, so I stand by what I say – you need to buy something to sell something.

Taxes

The one outgoing payment that many businesses overlook when planning is their tax bill. As described in an earlier chapter, there are several different sorts of tax that a business needs to pay and they are due at different times.

One reason for this oversight may be that HMRC does not necessarily send you a bill before the money is due, as a result it does not get scheduled and then there is a sudden call on funds.

Having said this, the payment dates are fixed and known potentially years in advance. It is only the exact amount that may not be known until just before it is due and this is the worse case scenario (PAYE is known once the payroll has been run for the month and VAT once the return has been completed). With other taxes you usually have more notice of the amount.

On a limited company set of accounts, it does state the corporation tax due. With an unincorporated business there is a bit more of an excuse for not knowing the exact figure as other factors may need to be taken into the calculation before the final tax payable figure is available to the business owner.

Whatever style of trading you use, you have no excuse for not knowing that tax has to be paid at some point. Plan for it.

Staff

Some business owners forget that there are several elements to payments for staff. The most straight forward being the net pay paid directly to the individual. The other amounts that need to be paid out should also be included in any calculation.

The elements will include tax and national insurance deducted from the employee's gross pay, plus employer's national insurance (covered in the chapter on taxes), any bonuses or commission due, pension contributions and then some of the hidden and often forgotten costs.

What are the terms and conditions of employment? Do your employees receive full pay if they are off ill? For how long can they receive full or half pay? As well as paying people who are away and not in a position to do their job, you may be having to pay for temporary or contract staff to cover their absence. This will add further to the costs.

What about maternity leave? Although you may be able to claim the money back from HMRC if you are a smaller employer, I have had one client where it took eighteen months before the repayment was received. It is possible to apply for an advance. If you are a smaller employer this may be well worth doing. Also consider what benefits the person on maternity leave is receiving. The small print in their contract or employment law may say that they need to carry on receiving their car allowance and pension payments at the full rate, even though they are not in the workplace.

The other staff related 'money out' is recruitment fees. If you use an agency to source new members of staff, this can add to the cost while saving you time. Look closely at the payment terms as payment is often required on the day the employee starts. When looking at the cost of a new member of staff, this can be a sizeable sum depending on the seniority of the appointment. There may be associated costs such as training courses, uniforms and providing a company vehicle. These expenses will very much depend on their role and your industry.

None of this is a problem providing you plan for the cash to go out.

Overheads

For the purposes of cash out, I am defining this as everything else your business needs to keep it running. This could be anything from the telephone and internet so that customers can place orders, to rent and rates so that you have somewhere for customers to come to, or for you to operate from.

With such a wealth of types of business, I am not going to try to list all the possibilities, only to suggest how you might create your own list.

Firstly, look at the payments you made last year and see whether they are all still relevant. Next, look at the accounts that were prepared for you by an external accountant and sent to HMRC. There may be headings on there where your accountant added in payments that you had paid for personally and not recharged to the business. Nonetheless, these were legitimate costs of running the business.

Next, go back through the last month to see where you and your staff have been and what they have done when they have been there. Have these activities incurred costs that have not been claimed back or put through expenses but could have been? Also, are you now doing things within the business that you were not doing last year, such as making payments for Google Adwords. If these are being paid via PayPal is that a business account or should someone be reimbursed by the business?

Before completing your list of what your business pays out, consider how often members of staff submit their expense claims. The worst I have seen is one claim for expenses for the past three years put in a single claim. Such a late claim is not helpful to the successful running of the business as profits have been calculated and taxes paid on what now turns out to be an incorrect figure. At worst, some of the expenses may have been due to be recharged to a customer that you no longer have. The funds can never be recovered. All staff should be encouraged to submit claims regularly and you may choose to introduce a rule that only claims made within six weeks of the expenditure being incurred will be paid. This certainly speeds up the staff's submission of claims.

When preparing this long list of monies that you are due to be paying out, it is worth putting a date due against each item, and a frequency.

Drawings /owner's account

Another 'money out' that often gets overlooked is money drawn out of the business by the director or owner.

It depends on the trading style as to how money should be withdrawn from the business.

One point to clarify is that if you are a sole trader, even if you call what you take out 'wages', it is only the withdrawal of your share of the profits. It is up to you to ensure you are making enough to take out at least the minimum wage – nobody else is going to top up the pot. Many business owners do not actually reach even this level for the hours they put in.

If you are a director and working in the business you should be on the payroll and therefore being paid a salary. The level of pay will depend on your contribution of time and effort, restricted by the ability of the business to pay. If the directors are also shareholders then dividends may also be allocated to them (see below). The other type of withdrawal by a director may be the repayment of any funds previously lent to the company by a director. These do not go through the payroll as they are simply loan repayments.

In general terms, if money is being drawn out either as cash or payments made on behalf of the business owner, it is not available for the business to use. You will know how much and when you need to take cash from the business. Although it is not necessarily an expense as such, make sure you include it in your calculations.

Dividends paid

Investors in a business will want to see some return and this is often by way of dividend payments. These were described in the chapter on reviewing your accounts.

These can only be paid where there is money in the business to do so. The challenge is that profits as shown in the accounts do not necessarily mean cash in the bank. You can say that you are giving a dividend (declaring a dividend), but it is the actual payment date that also needs to be recorded.

If you and your family members are the only shareholders, it may be that you have a paper transaction where the dividend is paid and immediately loaned back to the company. In this case no cash transaction is actually involved but if shareholders actually want cash, this needs to be planned for.

Repayment of loans

Whether the loan is due for repayment at monthly, quarterly or annual intervals, loans typically need repaying – and with interest.

In a similar way to taxes, the chances are that there is some documentation saying when and how much the repayments should be.

As this is not part of the trading of a business, this can often be overlooked when planning cash out. It is often a material figure with implications if not paid by the due date. It is therefore important that it is included.

The most likely repayment to be forgotten is where there is a balloon payment at the end of a contract. Although the monthly amounts are planned for, the final payment can often be considerable and even if the asset is then to be sold, the payment must be made before ownership can be transferred to make it available for sale.

I also include under this heading hire purchase and lease agreements. These are typically both monthly payments which need to be made by a particular date. Non or late payment of these will be recorded and can have significant effect on the acquisition of future loans so you need to ensure that there are sufficient funds for these types of payments.

Capital expenditure

This is one type of cash out that can be planned and controlled. It is the purchase of items of equipment, buildings, furniture and fittings that are due to be retained by the business for some time.

Part of their cost may be funded by way of loans or other types of finance, but in almost every case their purchase is optional.

One exception to this is where items are stolen or damaged and have to be funded before the insurance company pays up. Another is where the old one has broken beyond economic repair or the authorities will only let you continue to trade if you make certain alterations. The authorities I have in mind are the fire service and health and safety, to name two. In your industry you may know of more.

When planning any major expenditure you should always look beyond any apparent immediate need to ensure you do not adversely affect your longer term options. An example is building a single storey extension with footings that are only sufficient for a single storey. It may be that there is the opportunity to add a second storey at a later date. So are you better off having footings installed that would allow this rather than demolishing the single storey extension to build a taller one?

In the customer's bank account

One of the hidden users of cash is the invoice remaining unpaid by your customer. How much cash are you owed? Are you borrowing from your bank to pay the bills and paying your bank interest when your customers are taking interest free credit by not paying you on time?

Having a good system for credit control can make a difference to the profitability of your business. Not only are you saving time and effort by having a system in place, you will be reducing the chance of having to write off bad debts.

If your customers want extended credit you can review whether you can afford to support it and how much extra you will charge. Or, you can take the opposite view and start out with a higher standard price and discount for early payment. The thing to remember is that the longer your money stays in the customers' accounts, the less use you can put it to. Also, the more you may have to pay in interest to fund your other payments out.

Tied up in stock

In the same way that customers not paying you means you haven't got the cash, so you may have money not available as it is tied up in stock.

In reviewing your stock position you should consider the following factors. How much stock do you have which is obsolete, damaged or not current/slow moving? Is it still worth what you paid for it? How much is it costing you to store this stock?

I have seen clients who have a line of stock designed for a particular event which has not sold. They have then paid hundreds of pounds per month in storage costs for this stock that is no longer relevant because the event has passed. Even if they had given it to a clearance specialist for nothing within three months of recognising that they were not intending promote and sell it, they would have saved several thousand pounds in storage costs over the following twelve months.

As well as the cost of storage, the value of the stock should technically be the lower of the cost or how much you could get for it (net realisable value). If you reviewed your stock, would there be items that are past their sell by date or models that have been superseded? This easily happens in the computer industry where models change so fast.

When shedding old stock, consider which would be the best way to do it for the sake of your business. If you try and sell it at a discounted price to your customers, are you diverting their money to spend less with you than they would otherwise do? I pay less rent on my franking machine than I could have done as I asked about the ex-demonstration or older models they had lying around. It is still covered by a service contract and does the things I want it to do. You could say that at least the old machine is bringing in an income for them, or you could say they might have earned more from me by not telling me that this one was available. It is not always an easy decision.

The other factor in selling off old stock is the time it might take. I have one client who makes high value curtains, blinds and curtain rails. Once a year they have a one-day sale to clear out their stockrooms of cancelled orders, ends of rolls, ex-demonstration stock and anything else they don't need that is taking up space. It takes them a few days to prepare for the sale and it is manic on the day, but at the end of it they have space, money and know exactly what they have in stock going forward.

They dread that week, but know they will always feel good after the event.

KNOW YOUR CASH POSITION

Cash can change by the minute. Moving from having enough to cover the bills, to bounced direct debits incurring an unexpected charge can happen just like that. When a cheque you wrote some while ago is suddenly presented for clearance it can tip the balance. Thinking you have sufficient funds is not good enough.

How often do you update your books of account?

Whether it is you, a book-keeper or an accounts department doing the physical recording of information, you need to keep it as current as is practical. Once a month is not enough.

Keeping an eye on the true picture is key to the success of your business. You are then in a position to react quickly when the unexpected happens. An example follows relating to direct debits and this is not the first time it has happened to me. Failed direct debits can quickly and dramatically have an effect on your business' credit rating if unpaid. Treat them with respect.

I recently purchased a course priced at several thousand pounds where the payments were due to be drawn in three equal monthly amounts. The first payment went out as expected, the next day the direct debit claimed the full amount of the total course. Luckily there was enough in the account to cover the claim but I then had to phone the company to find out what had happened. It turned out they were new to direct debits and had got it wrong at their end. They immediately reimbursed my account with the amount taken in error and apologised. If I had not spotted this for three days, my payment to HMRC for VAT would not have gone out on the due date. I then could have had to pay HMRC surcharges due to the payment not being cleared. They would not have accepted the excuse that it was someone else's fault. I have also had the situation where HMRC took the VAT due for the quarter twice from my account. That took nearly two months to retrieve as someone had forgotten to set the flag to issue the repayment.

This highlights the fact that reviewing your cash is not just about seeing how close you are to plan, or whether the customers have kept their promises to pay, but also if anything unexpected has happened. It is easier to deal with it at the time rather than later when the consequences may have compounded the issues.

I recently worked with one firm where we put in place daily reporting to ensure they kept within the overdraft limit. The important factor was not just the balance each day, but to ensure that they had sufficient funds for the payroll, VAT and other large and occasional payments. One factor in this case was making sure that the process for daily reporting did not take up too much time and left capacity to continue running the business and collecting cash from the customers. What have you got in place within your business to monitor the cash?

Are you VAT registered?

If you are registered for VAT you will have a need to keep your books and records up to date at least quarterly. Even this is not often enough as this will not help you plan your expected cash flow with regard to your VAT payment. Although the final figure is not known until after the quarter end, you can watch the figure during the three months so you don't get any nasty surprises.

Depending on the size of your business, if the customers have paid you, the taxman will want part of what you have received – plan for it.

Do you pay staff?

One supplier, who will be very quick to complain if they do not get paid on time, is the supplier of labour to your business – the staff. They have given you their time in the expectation of being paid and you may feel it is a moral as well as a legal obligation to pay them.

What makes this worthy of specific comment is that you will have a good idea of the figure in advance, you know the date and you know the implications of not paying. The down side is that it is often a relatively large chunk of money towards the end of the month when customers are not due to pay you until after the date of the payroll. If you have staff, payroll happens every month or week so it should not come as a great surprise. If your employees are earning enough, you will also have another bill to pay by the middle of the following month, being the taxes deducted from their salaries and your contributions. This can therefore be added to the plan.

How often do you get paid for your invoices?

Just because you tell your customers when they need to pay does not mean that is when they will pay. I know this seems obvious but I would ask you to remember it when you are looking at what is due in and when.

The other situation to spot is when customers have not paid you for an extended period. Is there a problem with the invoice, the goods or service or the customer's cash flow? You need to find this out so it can be dealt with even if it results in agreed payment terms for them to clear the old invoice. I expect you would rather have some money than none and once they start to pay, they are confirming that they owe the money in the court's eyes as well as yours. Taking customers to court will cost you some money, and some time not being paid may cost you a lot more.

WHY PROFIT IS NOT CASH

From the section above it might be starting to dawn on you that just because you have raised a sales invoice, it does not mean that you have cash in the bank.

If you have been with the business since it started up, then you will appreciate that there were expenses you had to pay out either before, or very soon after, you got your first customer. Where did that money come from? At its simplest, if your business is a limited company, then someone had to pay Companies House to set the company up and register it before it could bring in any income.

Although some of these expenses can be offset against sales to work out the profit, that is not the same as what you have or haven't got in the bank.

If you buy and sell goods, the calculation of profit will include the cost of the goods sold, not the cost of goods purchased. To demonstrate with a simple but extreme example, you buy £100 of goods and don't sell any during the year; your sales are nil, your cost of items sold is nil, therefore your profit is nil, but your cash position is minus £100, being the money you had to spend out on stock. You will understand from the last section that you can't use the money for anything else as it is tied up in stock. You may be able to borrow some more to help promote your business and create sales to free up cash, but you will still have to pay that back.

This may seem an extreme example, but it can happen in practice for a particular line of stock where the wrong size is purchased and just sits there, or no effort is put into marketing a new line and therefore no sales are made. This can happen where the business is started as a sideline and then not enough time is found to promote the business. It brings to mind a client who thought her salaried position was about to come to an end so she put lots of effort into the business she had started a couple of years before. She had initially purchased stock and stored it in the house. She kept living with the stock but not aggressively promoting the part-time business.

After a couple of years, as a result of this increased threat of losing her salary, she focused on making money from the business. She made a profit and surprised herself. She learned not only where her customers could be found but, more importantly, the types of products they would buy from her. Since then she has become much more aware of purchasing decisions and the cost of carrying stock you are not selling. Her employment contract has been extended but she also feels much happier that she makes money from her part-time business now that she is much more selective about her buying decisions.

The biggest killer when your money is not available as cash is the taxman. He calculates how much you have to pay on paper, not on a cash basis. There is the suggestion that smaller businesses will be able to work on a cash basis. This should mean if they make a profit, they can afford to pay the taxman. An example of where there is currently a problem is when a very big sale is made just before the end of the year. The sales and profits for the year look good, but by the time the tax is due, the customer you sold to has gone out of business and has not paid you. Although this bad debt can be used to reduce next year's profit, it technically cannot be used as an excuse for not paying the tax bill. In practice you can try pleading your case but it will not stop interest and potential penalties building up on the non payment of tax.

In the case of Value Added Tax, you can elect to work on a cash basis. This means you work out how much VAT to pay based on sales that you have been paid for by customers and payments you have made to suppliers. Payment of VAT is not based on profits but I thought it relevant to include the one tax that currently recognises that cash is not linked to paper transactions, particularly for the smaller business.

Cash from Sales

Part of your profit will be calculated with reference to sales. If customers pay you before or at the point of sale, that is fine, you have the money.

However if they expect to pay you after they receive the invoice, you will not have the cash although the sale has been made. It is dependent on your terms and how well your customers stick to your terms as to when you can expect the money in.

Payment terms out

To calculate the profit, the allowable expenses need to be deducted from sales. If you have to pay up front for your goods, this will eat up the cash that you haven't necessarily had in. The worst case for this is where you might have services such as labour which you have to pay for before the job is complete, but the taxman will still calculate profit by looking at how much work you have done and how much that would sell for, even if you haven't raised the invoice yet. In the case of my accountancy practice this may be preparing accounts and preparing tax returns but as the client has not yet answered the outstanding queries, I do not view the job as complete so have not yet sent the bill. I have, however, paid my staff and the rent and my travel costs to see the client, to name but a few costs where the cash has gone out already.

The taxman will expect me to put a value on the work in progress and then tax me on the profits even though I have not issued the invoice. This is why it is so important to keep an eye on the figures so the cash is there for the tax bill, which is one supplier you can be sure has a computer programme to work out interest on late payments by the day.

Adjustments for capital items

If you have spent your cash buying long term items, only a part will be used as an expense against sales to work out the profit. As the items are expected to last for several years, the cost will be spread over this period. The fact is that all the cash was paid in year one. This is another example of why profit does not equal available funds – you have spent it on something which will also be around next year, and the year after.

Drawings

If you are operating as a sole trader or partnership then you may well be taking cash out of the business to live on. That is fine but it is the share of profits that you are helping yourself to. The profit will be calculated without including any wages for you or any other partners. Any payments that have been made on your behalf but are not required for the business, such as paying for your holiday, may have taken up available cash but are not part of the profit calculation.

Sometimes a notional salary may be included for management and planning purposes but the taxman will take it out again when deciding how much tax you have to pay.

How to release cash

Having described where your cash might be lurking I have already described some ways in which cash can be released, but what follows is a recap of these.

Better payment terms

What would it take for customers to pay with the order if they do not do so already? If this is not practical, can they pay on receipt of goods or service? If this is not possible what do you do to ensure customers pay on the day they are due to pay? What penalties are there for late payments?

Longer credit terms

Review your suppliers. Have you ever enquired about credit accounts with your suppliers? Some companies are more than happy to give you a credit account for two reasons. Firstly, it cuts down on their paperwork just having one payment a month from you. Secondly, they may well take the view that they establish some form of loyalty. This may be because you think they are a good supplier and therefore your supplier of choice or, it is easier and less fiddly if you don't need to pay as you go.

If you do want to delay payment, always talk to the supplier first and get their agreement. It is not just that you may want to use them again, but because you want to preserve your credit history. Remember, even if you are struggling to pay the whole amount, most people would rather receive some money and a promise of more, than none.

Sell stock

As discussed above, it is easy to keep money tied up in stock, and you may have the cost of storage as well. Do a stock take and see what you could shift to allow you to focus on going forward: eBay is one route and you can put a minimum price on items. Remember that there will be PayPal charges and postage costs that you need to deduct from the money you eventually receive. If the types of goods you sell don't fit in the post, there is always freight or buyer collects. Freeads and other magazine-based outlets are also a possibility, or clearance magazines or companies that will give you not a lot, but you will save the cost of storage and it will free up the space.

Don't spend too much time trying to be too clever otherwise any money you make will be less than what you could have made by investing your time elsewhere.

Whatever method you use it is also worth reviewing why the stock had not sold at full price previously to ensure you do not find yourself in the same position in six months time.

Sell and lease back

Depending what buildings, equipment and vehicles you have within your business, another method of raising funds is to sell and lease back the asset. There are companies that specialise in these types of agreements.

Do remember that in the long term it will cost you substantially more than if you had just kept ownership of the asset, but if it allows growth which will net you an even greater amount, this could be a good way forward.

If you take this route, you are not alone. The government in the UK has done this with some of their buildings and the NHS has been criticised for doing exactly this and costing the country extra millions over the next 25 years. The fact is that it has freed up cash in the short term and allowed them to schedule costs going forward that do not include the upkeep of the buildings, as that is part of what the leaseback fees cover.

HOW OFTEN SHOULD YOU REVIEW YOUR CASH POSITION?

This will depend on how large your business is, how accurate your plans are and how much flexibility you have.

If you are operating close to your overdraft limit, then I would suggest reviewing daily. If you have a little more flexibility, then do it weekly. Leaving it to once a month is fine if someone else is doing the weekly check.

Part of the check is going to be that cash has come in from customers. Leaving it a month after the due date before chasing them runs the risk of them increasing their debt and therefore using your money to run their business. That might be fine if you are making them pay for the privilege.

Credit control is therefore a vital part of any business. Even if you receive cash before the order, reviewing the cash in allows you to ensure you have the capacity to deal with the sales and avoid the need for refunds.

If you have a good accounts team to monitor these things, this does not negate your involvement. Having a monthly figure of what bills are to be paid and who is due to pay you, will allow you to consider the optional extras you are aware of but have not yet reached the accounts department. Also, if the projected cash flow is adverse, you can work with the accounts department to decide on the best route forward.

How often do you do payment runs?

When do your suppliers want to be paid? Some may be cash with order, in which case that is simple, there are others with which you may have an account. Have you read the small print? Some will say net 30 days which is taken to mean 30 days after the end of the month within which the invoice is dated. Others may be seven days from the invoice date. If you only do payment runs once a month, are you going to incur penalties, upset your suppliers or be put on stop if you only pay once a month?

Whatever system you use, you should always know how much you owe, when it is due and when you intend to pay.

WHO NEEDS TO KNOW?

To date, I have referred to the need for you as the business owner to know where the cash comes from and goes to. The truth is others are interested in the cash as well as the profit.

Business owner

As the business owner or the manager responsible, the duty of care rests with you. Even if you have an accounts team they should know that you are interested and keep you informed.

If you can foresee the need for extra cash, even for a short period, you need to make the decisions as to where that money is coming from and how much you are prepared to pay to get it. Many years ago, I was considering applying for a £500 overdraft but with the arrangement fees and admin fees, the charges were going to be £500. If you think about these figures, if I had taken up the offer, the overdraft of £500 would have been used to pay the bank charges and fees, making me no better off. When questioned, the bank did say that perhaps I had better have a £1,000 facility. I chose not to take them up on their offer and used my personal credit card as I knew it was only a short term requirement. The fact was that it was an informed decision.

Banks

Another party who may be interested is your banker. One reason they may make the request is not that they want to know the figures, but they want to make sure you know the figures. I have known situations where the bank requires monthly reports by fifteenth of each month, but through the wonders of technology I could see that the attachments to the emails containing the figures were not being opened until just before the quarterly meeting with the client. What the bank manager did know was that each month the figures were being prepared.

Investors

Your investors may be very interested in the cash flow position. They will not necessarily be interested in the individual amounts but if they have offered staged payments, they will want to know how you have used their money so far and when you will need the next tranche.

They will also want to know that you are taking care of the money they have invested to date. It depends on the agreement as to how formal their involvement might be but at least if you offer, they know you care and have nothing you are trying to hide.

Staff

You might ask why staff want to know. If your sales people are paid commission or a bonus based on customers paying their bills rather than just the invoice being raised, it will focus their minds on making the sale as clean as possible. The sales people will form part of the credit control team as they want to be paid their commission.

Other staff may need to know as to when they can place orders as they don't want to work out schedules only to find the business is on stop and one supplier refuses to deliver, which prevents the whole job being started although all other suppliers have delivered and will want paying.

Managing cash is something that managers are not often taught. I have seen marketing managers book exhibition space and be surprised when accounts complain that they have suddenly got to find x thousand pounds although the event is not for another year. If the marketing manager considered when the cash was due out, they would realise that 95% of the expenditure for a show typically happens between the booking date and a month before. Sales as a result of the event are between the actual date and six months forward, depending on the buying cycle in the particular industry.

What figures you choose to share is up to you, but sharing those where the staff can have some impact makes them feel empowered as well as spreading the load and taking some of it off your shoulders.

Other lenders

If others are going to lend you money they will want to know that you can afford the repayments.

The common example I have in mind is a leasing company. They tend to want to make a few enquiries before they say 'sign here'. If you have made sure your books are kept up to date for your benefit and you have a good idea about your business finances, you can inspire the lender with confidence that you have your finger on the pulse.

Another lender I have dealt with is HMRC. I was able to put a payment plan in place for outstanding VAT which was seasonally adjusted as most of the company's sales were made in the autumn. By producing historic figures to demonstrate the trends of cash flow and future plans to show the affordability, the owner was able to get a stay of execution rather than having the company put into liquidation.

Board of directors

If there are multiple owners and managers of the business they should all be interested in the financial position. It may be that they are also investors or just responsible for a particular area. Whatever the case, whether the business currently has enough cash and is in a good position to go forward and expand or cash is extremely tight, this should influence how each one plans the future of the area for which they are responsible.

You often hear that the finance director is responsible and therefore no one needs to worry. You can end up in a circle where nobody asks or challenges the figures, the finance director thinks no-one is interested and doesn't share the information so everyone assumes it is fine and there is no need to worry.

Every manager and director can make a difference, whether

it is the sales director reviewing the type of customers that the business looks for and under what terms they can take them on, the operations director looking at the delivery times or the fulfilment of contracts, the marketing director understanding the returns on investments from various campaigns, or the human resource director looking at staffing and deciding whether more or fewer staff are needed.

If you are a small organisation, you may find you occupy all these posts. It is even more important that you don't just leave it to your book-keeper. They are employed to record transactions, potentially collect cash and pay suppliers. They do not know enough about the strategic direction of the business and forthcoming plans to have a complete picture unless, of course, you share it all with them.

Summary

A business cannot survive without cash. Understanding how to get it and where it goes to is the key to business success. Designing a plan is a good start but you also need to monitor the situation and update the plan.

By now you will understand that just because you have a profit doesn't mean that there is more in the bank. This knowledge will enable you to plan your funds so you can make the most of every opportunity, knowing that if you spend money you know when the cash returns are likely to be seen.

Having spent money on this book, and taken the time to read it, I would expect you to save at least an hour of your accountant's time which is cash you won't need to find.

In all honesty, I expect you to be able to make/save much more than that by managing your cash as well as your profit.

7 Problems don't go away if you do nothing

One reason for writing this book is that some clients, and prospective clients have come to me for help after they have done something they shouldn't have, but didn't know any better. It may be getting involved with invoice finance, it may be asking me to do the payroll but then not actually paying the staff due to lack of funds. So many problems can be dealt with differently if you take action early enough.

By understanding the figures you can start to realise problems may be approaching and tackle them before it is too late to do anything.

My hope is that by realising the accounts are a useful tool and not a page of a language that means nothing to you, you will want to look at them and take action. Even if your conclusion is you need help with translation, seeking help is a step in the right direction.

Problems compound

Problems not tackled can compound. A simple example is not paying HMRC. If you do not have the money to settle a bill by the due date, you can talk to them and may be able to negotiate payment terms. Yes, you will still need to pay interest but will avoid penalties, which would just be giving money to the government for nothing. If you would like to give money to the government, I am sure you would rather do it as tax on the large profits you are making rather than penalties for mismanagement of your funds.

The same logic can apply to suppliers. Paying them nothing when the statement comes through increases the chance of being put on stop and damaging your credit rating. Paying something, confirms to them that you acknowledge the debt and reassures them that you are trying your best.

The worst client I have had for paying interest and bank charges was a new client in 2006. The business had paid bank charges and interest of just over £3,000 on a turnover of £23,000. By 2007 it was down to £357 on a similar turnover. You may ask how this could be. The answer was simple. When suppliers pressed them to pay the outstanding amounts, a cheque was written and sent with no regard to whether there were funds available to pay. The business was therefore getting a bounced cheque fee each time the cheque was presented, plus interest when the charges were added to the overdraft.

So, in one year, the profit increased by over £2,500 simply by stopping the writing of cheques and instead, talking to suppliers. They also stopped placing orders until the money was available. In fact the first year the business worked with me, it more than doubled its profits without increasing its turnover. Since then, the owner understands the figures and runs a lean but profitable business... and they can sleep at night.

PROBLEMS HAVE KNOCK-ON EFFECTS

As I referred to above, one of the frustrating events is when you find you are put on stop and you didn't know that there was even a chance it could happen. If you are to make continued sales, you need to ensure that you have continued supplies.

If you have a customer waiting to pay you on delivery of goods, you don't want to find you lose the customer as you can't deliver when promised because your supplier won't release the goods. At worst, the supplier releases the goods late and the customer has already gone elsewhere and you are left with having to pay for the goods and no customer waiting to pay you.

Another problem that can catch you out is when your service providers have a problem collecting payment. This may be due to you changing your bank, or simply that your card has been replaced and your old card number stored in the service provider's system or PayPal is no longer valid. If this is the provider of your phone system, how much business and goodwill might you have lost before you put it right?

GOOD PROBLEMS AS WELL AS BAD

Are you getting lots of new business but are unable to supply them to the level of service you would wish? Have you got your bank manager calling to suggest that as you have so much money in the current account, you should think about moving some to a different account? Is one of your competitors retiring and offering you their business for a very reasonable sum?

In all cases you could just carry on as if nothing has happened, but would that really be the best for your business? To lose existing customers because you cannot service the greater number you now have? To ignore the bank manager's phone calls because you think it must be bad news – that is why bank managers phone, isn't it?

You might miss the opportunity to acquire another business – or at least find out more – and let another one of your competitors take over the retiring business owner's customers. The agreement may be to settle over a number of years as a percentage of sales from them with only a minimal up front cost for drawing up the agreement.

Knowing where you are now and where you have come from puts you in a much better position to make the correct decision fast and seize the opportunity to act before it is gone or the situation becomes a negative – see above.

Problems can close the business

I have mentioned above the consequences of not paying some of your service providers such as telephone, website and other hosted services.

If customers and suppliers cannot get hold of you they may start to worry and take disproportionate action.

Whether you are a sole trader, partnership or a limited company, there are ways that suppliers and customers can start action to close you down.

The problem with this sort of action is it can take much more time effort and money to stop the action than to prevent it starting.

At its simplest, the moment a supplier applies to the courts for an unsettled debt there are court fees incurred which they will expect to recover from you. As with the penalties to HMRC, why pay them if you can avoid it?

If you do not respond to the court papers, you will automatically be found guilty of non payment and a payment order made. If this is not paid, a County Court Judgement (CCJ) can be granted and the bailiffs sent in. If there are insufficient funds, then an application can be made to bankrupt the individual or liquidate the company. This can be done for a debt as small as £750 as things stand today.

To start fighting your corner at this stage can become very costly as well as the damage to your reputation.

If you had spoken to the supplier you owed money to (your creditor) and either cleared up any issues regarding missing invoices, faulty goods or simple late payment, it would have taken action on your part but it would have been cheaper, more pleasant and less time consuming than the alternative.

I have just detailed the problems that are financially based. There are others, such as not complying with health and safety, that are outside the remit of this book, but the same rule applies. If you ignore an improvement order, your business may be in jeopardy.

THE LONG TERM IMPACT

Closing the business is terminal. But assuming the business survives there are other long term impacts from ignoring problems.

Interest and charges

If you plan for short term funding but ignore the fact it has to be paid back, it can be frightening how much interest you are charged in the year.

Many business owners look to credit cards for short term finance, but even if they are interest free for the first x months, if you do not repay them or transfer them on to a cheaper form of lending, you are again paying money out of the business that you do not need to.

If you are operating with an overdraft, talk to the bank and see if it would be cheaper to convert it to a loan. Yes, you would need to repay the loan but this may not be much more than the difference between overdraft interest and loan interest. Unless you investigate you will not know.

CCJ

Not everyone realises the cost of having a CCJ. Once it is on your, or your business', record it stays there for six years. In some industries, it may affect your legality to operate. In all cases it will affect the cost, and potentially opportunities, of borrowing in future.

They are best avoided and one way is to make sure you talk to anyone you owe money to and, if you cannot pay straight away, sort out a payment plan. If there is a dispute, then try to resolve it rather than go to court as it is much cheaper.

If it is your customers who haven't paid you, again, the quicker you can chase them, the more chance you have of getting paid. Consider accepting payment terms from them as, even if they stop before the end, you have some money rather than none.

ACTION YOU CAN TAKE IF YOU ARE RUNNING OUT OF MONEY

If you simply have not got the funds to pay when payments are due, there are things you can do other than bury your head in the sand.

Time to pay

As I have discussed above, everyone would rather have some money rather than none, even the taxman. You should not use it as a ploy to confuse any court papers by paying some so the debt being chased is wrong. This was an old trick that the courts are now more aware of and will accept that the debt has been partly repaid but the action can go ahead on the rest.

As soon as you start to pay you are acknowledging the debt. I had one client who I took to court and over a six month period she challenged each bill individually and, as she had to accept the work was done, it was a reasonable charge and she had no choice but to pay it. She even challenged bills she had previously paid claiming I had overcharged her. When it went to court all her claims were thrown out and she was ordered to pay all of the amounts due and court costs. It took me over two weeks chargeable time to deal with her continuing requests and preparation for court. If she had said I will pay you £200 per month until the outstanding amount is clear, she would have saved herself around £400 as well as her time. The debt would have been settled by the same date.

If your supplier denies your request for staged payments, point out the costs to them and their time of pursuing the claim.

Supplementing the income

If your business has insufficient income to pay its bills, one of which may be a 'living' wage for you, then one option is to see what else can be done.

The first question is, does it only need to be in the short term to get over a hiccup, or do other options need considering? See the next section.

If it is a short term issue, you may be in a position to sub-let part of your premises. I would suggest that you check on the rental agreement, but providing you ensure that the net effect is that there will be more income without more cost, then this could help tide you over. I have seen clients that have included using their card machine as part of the services provided to a tenant but forgotten there are processing costs, time for the cash to reach their account and insurance issues. All of these may not be what you are actually after when looking for rental income.

Another form of income to support the business is where the business owner does some freelance work for others. If they have the skill but cannot get the business, this can be another way to bring in money without closing the business.

Another option, if no others exist, is to find part time employment where you don't have to think too hard. The reason I phrase it like this is I had one client who suggested also offering a decorating service to supplement their unconnected business. The challenge with this was that they would need to market and manage the service in the same way they did their other business. They would need to continually get new customers.

If you are going to take on anything else it needs to involve turning up, doing the 'job' and then leaving. When I had a large amount unpaid by a client and had to do something to keep the cash coming in, I worked at a call centre. Not the best paid work but it was a few evenings a week which did not distract me from my business and brought in a regular amount each month until I sorted out the cash flow problems. I also used it as a learning opportunity for selling on the phone. Make the most of what is presented to you.

Liquidation and other options

If you decide that it is impossible to carry on there are a variety of options. It is worth getting independent advice as the chances are you are too close to the situation to make a clear decision. Even if you are not quite at this stage, talk to someone else as they will be in a position to think straight.

One option may be to sell the business. Even if it cannot pay its bills and has made a loss in the last year, someone may have an interest in what you do have, so do not give up and assume it is worthless.

With most registered liquidators, the first initial chat is often free. They can advise you. The aim should be to make it less painful for you, their client. They may not have good news, but at least it will be an honest and professional opinion. You may choose a second opinion. If they say the same, they are probably correct.

SUMMARY

To end this section on a more positive note, my message is don't ignore problems, treat them as challenges. There is always something that can be done and there is more choice the earlier you act.

A problem shared is a problem halved. By talking to someone else about it, they may be able to help you generate ideas that you can't see because you are too close to the issue.

Before deciding on your way forward, make sure you have collected all the facts so you can put a current issue into the wider context of the business. Don't just put a bucket under the drip; make sure you know where the water is coming from so you can fix that.

8 Look to the future

The standing joke when I started accountancy in the 1970s was why did the accountant cross the road? Because he did it last year.

There are different types of accountants and they will focus on different areas of the numbers. The most common type that smaller business owners meet are those that produce accounts based on historic information for the benefit primarily of the tax man. A copy is also available for the investors and the business owner. This is not a criticism, as that is all many small business owners think is required. You are different.

The purpose of this book is to help you understand the historic figures as this will give you better control of your future. The future you can do something about, it is too late to do anything about the past – except learn from it.

GOALS AND TARGETS

You need to decide what goals you have for you and your organisation. Whatever size it is at the moment, you cannot expect to do nothing and expect to get what you want.

Like any journey, without a destination and milestones you will not know which direction to travel in and whether you are on the right path.

My next book goes into much more detail as to the targets you need to set for different areas, how to build them into your plan and the financial implications of what you want to do.

Without knowing what you want, it is difficult to be sure what funds you will need to do it. If you are going to need to source funding from loans or investors, they will want to know what your plan is for the short and the long term.

You can add up the sales invoices issued in the year and feel you know what your turnover is historically. But there is more to planning and projections than stating that you want to grow sales by 10%. What implications are there for the other aspects of the business, for the cash required to fund the growth, for the staff you will need to deliver this increase?

CREATING THE PLANS

Once you know what you want to achieve, there are two plans that you need to create which contain numbers. Each of these will benefit from having historic figures to work from.

If you are new to business and have no history yet, there are other sources that will be of benefit rather than starting with a totally blank sheet.

Don't put off making a plan just because you do not have enough information. Once you start the plan you will see what further information you need so that it can be completed.

The other important fact about a plan is that it can be changed. Whether it is your decision or factors beyond your control, the possibility of change should not prevent you from starting.

If you set out on a journey and know the route and when you expect to get there, you don't stay at home just because there may be road works that no-one has told you about. So it is in business, until you start the journey you don't know what you may need to change. The important thing is that you know where you are trying to get to.

For any successful business there are two types of plans that are inter-related. These are covered in detail in the next book. For now, an explanation will help.

Budgets

Budgets are predictions of the future, usually prepared for one or more years. The years nearest to now, may well be divided further into months, and can go as fine as weeks, depending on the business. Later years may be left as single periods of twelve months, if prepared at all.

The budget will look similar to a trading and profit and loss account with sales and cost of sales following through to expenses. Where a single payment relates to the whole year, for example insurance, a twelfth would be shown each month. Rent paid quarterly would be treated in a similar way with the quarter's payment being divided by three, and one month's cost being entered against each month.

Depending on what planning is being done, a budget can also be prepared for some balance sheet items. This would typically apply to vehicles, equipment and other large sales and purchases that can be recognised. Budgets can be prepared for all figures, but that is another book.

Cash flow

This report allows the business to plan when cash is expected to come in and go out. It is not a budget.

Many business owners try and combine the two. They are not the same. You pay your car tax once a year; you need to plan to have the cash available the month it has to be paid. This is cash flow. You get the benefit from the car tax for twelve months; a budget would show one twelfth each month.

One term that is bandied about which gives rise to the confusion is when people refer to a budgeted cash flow. What they actually mean is a planned cash flow or projected cash flow. My next book goes into much more detail about the preparation of the cash flow and how to use it.

www.understanding-accounts.co.uk/book2

OTHER PEOPLE THAT ARE AFFECTED

As the business owner, the future is in your hands and affects you, but remember there is also an impact on others.

Staff

Having reviewed the accounts for last year and understood how your business finances are working (or not) it is time to make plans so that you can ensure you have the right staff in place.

If you already have staff, are they going to need further training? Are there tools or systems and processes that you can put in place so that they can work more efficiently and enjoy their work? You might think the idea of enjoying work is strange, but if your employees are enjoying their work, think how much more they are willing to contribute to the business. I don't simply mean unpaid overtime, but the whole ethos which customers and suppliers perceive will differentiate you from others in your market.

As a customer, would you prefer to deal with an individual who is relaxed and wanting to help serve you, or someone who is counting the minutes until the end of their working day? This is the sort of action and attitude that customers really notice.

If employees know what your plans are, they can help you work towards them. They will have a sense of purpose and direction that can support you as well as the business.

Lenders

If you have anyone lending the business money, they may want to know what your plans are for the coming years, how secure their loan is and the likelihood that you may want further funding for growth.

Having plans in place will give them confidence that you are in control and can give them adequate notice allowing you to get a better deal than suddenly knocking on the door announcing you need the money in 24 hours.

Customers

Repeat business is always good as it is the cheapest to obtain. I appreciate that in some industries the chances are slim, as people don't tend to buy a swimming pool that often, or arrange their will on a regular basis. However, if the customers are happy with your service they will refer you to other people looking for the same goods or services.

If you have plans for the future they may include a referral fee or introducer's token. Sharing these plans with established customers may help increase your business but, if it is a while since you spoke to them, they may wish to have an update on where you are now and where you are going.

Even customers to whom you provide a continuing service will be interested to know how this might be improved or extended. Existing customers are often a forgotten source of extra income, as well as ideas.

You owe it to yourself

Even if you have had goals before but not met them, or have wildly exceeded them, it doesn't matter. You can learn what went according to plan and what didn't, which factors you had not taken into account and which factors were irrelevant.

Don't be put off by plans made but never referred to. Check out the summary figures now and see what was different and, when you next make plans, how you need to do them differently. My first suggestion would be to actually check against the plan. Whether this is done within your accounts software or by way of a spreadsheet the method is not critical, taking action is.

Without a plan, you will have to deal with the unexpected, be working in the dark and for an unknown outcome. I am not advocating that every business needs a 60 plus page business plan with everything in minute detail. Even a one-page outline and a one-page budget with a one-page cash flow may be more than you have now.

If you already have and work with more than this, well done, you are on your way to success. Having read this book, it may be that you understand it better, but there is still more to learn.

CONCLUSION

While writing this chapter I am resisting the urge to expand further. The second book was originally part of this one, but I felt that I had even more to say than would fit in a book that a busy owner would think of reading.

In breaking business success down into stages, the first and most important stage is to understand the numbers. Once you understand what the numbers mean, and that they are useful and not just for accountants, you can use that knowledge to plan going forward and make decisions that will lead to the success of your business.

Putting plans in place is progress towards ultimate success, but the third stage will make all the difference. This third stage is to act and monitor. Having a plan is all very well, but if you don't follow it, or notice when you are going off track, and take corrective action, you will not reach your goal. This then takes you back to understanding what has happened, what was good and what was bad – and how things could be improved.

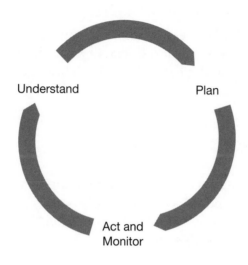

Look out for my next book to understand and feel confident about business plans, budgets and cash flow forecasting in the same way that you now have a better understanding of your accounts.

My suggestion to you is to go online and register your interest in the next book. You will then find that you may be eligible for a discount against the full price.

www.understanding-accounts.co.uk/book2

The End
Until the next time …